Born to Sail

ON OTHER PEOPLE'S BOATS

JENNIFER P STUART

SHERIDAN HOUSE

For Greg, for so many reasons.

ACKNOWLEDGMENTS

Many thanks to David Hildred, who helped with the technical editing and graciously offered his comfortable boat *Serai* as hotel and model cruising yacht.

Thank you, Neal Steiger, Professor, New Hampshire Technical College, who patiently untangled my tangled punctuation and tenses.

Thanks also to the editors at Sheridan House, who untangled the rest of the tangle.

Thank you Mary and Charlie Swain, whose efforts are not visible but appreciated just the same.

And to all my friends who thought I was crazy but cheered me on anyway, thanks for your much needed support!

First published 1991 by
Sheridan House Inc.
145 Palisade Street
Dobbs Ferry, NY 10522

Copyright © 1991 by Jennifer P Stuart

Library of Congress Cataloging-in-Publication Data

Stuart, Jennifer P
    Born to sail—on other people's boats / Jennifer P Stuart.
       p.   cm.
    ISBN 0-924486-11-2
    1. Sailboat living.   2. Yachts and yachting.   3. Seamanship.
    I. Title.
    GV811.65.S78   1991
    797.1'24'023—dc20   91-7214
                                                                                CIP

Cover, design and illustrations by Jeremiah B. Lighter

Printed in the United States of America

ISBN 0-924486-11-2

CONTENTS

2

Born to Sail

I was born to sail. I didn't know that I was—not for many years. Nowhere in my family background have I detected a single seafarer. True, my grandparents on my mother's side came over on the boat from Sicily, and grandfather opened a fishmarket in New Jersey—but I didn't even eat fish until I was in my late 20s.

By age 29, although I had started eating fish, I still hadn't figured out what it was I was born to do. So I tried a few different careers. First, professional secretarial work. Then office management. Then advertising copy writing. Then public relations. And, finally, technical writing. None of these careers really suited me. They were just jobs I did while waiting for something exciting to happen. But nothing did—until I took my first sailing lesson.

I started on the San Francisco Bay in a little 22-foot ramshackle hull I nicknamed "The Garbage Scow." It wasn't long before I graduated to sleek 30-foot sloops, then to 40-footers. I sailed in rain, on cold, choppy waves in gusty 25-knot winds, in bright sun with warm, gentle 15-knot breezes. I experienced knockdowns in strong winds. I fought the wheel to keep the boat on course while getting drenched with icy, polluted Bay water. I saw fabulous sunrises and gentle sunsets. I stood the helm for eleven solid hours on my first open-ocean trip when the crew got seasick and I was the last body standing. It was my first taste of life on a boat outside the Bay, and my desire to sail the world took hold.

Additional sailing experience included two weeks in the British Virgin Islands on a bareboat charter. The sailing conditions were ideal. I lived, and could have died, fulfilled—clothed in nothing more than a bikini, wearing a mask and snorkel for accessories. I had the sun on my skin, the warm winds in my hair, and a gently rocking deck under my ten bare toes.

And, finally, I sailed for two weeks in the Society Islands in the South Pacific on another two-week bareboat charter. I almost never left the boat. I soaked up the sun and drowsed with the waves gently lapping the hull. I bathed in the fresh wind and counted the coconut palms and banana trees that lined the shore. And just before it was time to come back home, I experienced the exhilarating rollercoaster fun of twelve-foot seas and 35-knot winds on the crossing from Huahine to Raiatea—and I knew if I did not soon get on a sailboat permanently I would lose my will to live. But I did not own a boat. At that time, as now, I knew I never would.

Even with my years of sailing experience, I still could not accurately name every item or point of sail on a sailboat. Nor did I know navigation. But I could hoist and trim the sails, keep the bow just off the wind to maintain hull speed, tack before hitting something, and perform a controlled jibe when the winds got crazy. Luckily, I never got seasick, no matter what the conditions. In addition, I was getting a glimpse of foreign waters and different cultures which I knew were only the icing on the cake. When my marriage ended, my time to sail the seas had arrived.

At 36 I decided to crew my way around the world. Within a year I had sold my house and everything in it, packed only what I could carry in a seabag, and headed for Greece to find my first crewing position on an oceangoing sailboat.

This book is offered to those of you who have not yet determined what you were born to do, no matter what your age. Its purpose is to pave the way for you into a life that could offer you exciting challenges, along with peace of mind, body and spirit—just in case those windowless conference rooms, the daily traffic jams, and the mounting bills make you question the meaning of life, too.

I left it all behind. I was born to sail.

FOR THE SHIP'S LOG

1

1

Untangle Your Tangle

First, a trial run: You need to experience living aboard a sailboat, preferably offshore, for at least two weeks. Visit your nearest marina and test the process of finding a crewing position. Pick up one of the publications that are handed out for free at most marinas and aimed at the boating crowd. Check the ads, and place one yourself. Ask sailing questions of strangers. Try a crewed charter, or become part of a boat delivery crew yourself. Those would be two excellent tests of your commitment to the sailing lifestyle.

Once you've decided to venture forward and never to look back—untangle, distribute, sell, let go, and clean out. Be brutal. After all, getting away from the old lifestyle is the whole idea. When you gear your mind toward a total change, you'll surprise yourself with what you can live comfortably without, and how fast you can pay off your outstanding bills when you stop buying more unnecessary landlubber stuff.

Start with where you live. If you rent, you can walk away. If you own, you can sell and walk away, or find someone to manage the house until you decide whether or not you are coming back. While gearing down your lifestyle, find a comfortable room to rent or share rent with a friend in less expensive accommodations for a while to cut your biggest expenses. I found one room in a friend's three bedroom/two bath house and spent less than half the amount on rent per month than my former monthly mortgage payment. Check your local newspapers for rooms to rent, ask friends to ask their friends, and check with your local realtors. You'll be surprised how well you can live on much less.

If you decide to sell your house, be sure to research the tax laws in your state regarding capital gains and the rules of reinvesting. A good tax consultant or lawyer can help you with this. You can invest the bulk of the profits in a long-term, high-yield account, or in stocks. There are many investment packages from which to choose. Remember, plan the sale and your investments carefully. Talk with an investment counselor and a tax specialist to determine the best return on your money. I invested half the profits in long-term high-yield whatevers, and put the rest in short-term Certificate of Deposit accounts to have on hand should I need them—which I didn't.

What is most important is to do what gives you peace of mind. Sell out, travel, and never look back. Or find someone to manage your property while you are traveling and deciding if you are coming back. The choice is yours.

Now, about your job. If you're convinced you'll be heading out to a sailing life and never looking back, just quit your job when you're ready to leave and walk away. However, if you feel more secure trying the lifestyle before abandoning all that is familiar, perhaps it would be best to take a leave of absence from your job for two months minimum, six months maximum. While you're gone, you might find something out there in the world that you like doing better.

After spending about 20 years enclosed in corporate office walls, I decided to quit and never look back—even if it meant slinging hamburgers should the sailing life not turn out to float my boat. I haven't slung a hamburger yet.

IMPORTANT NOTE

Be sure that the person you find to handle your house and bills is responsible. If you don't have a truly reliable resource to depend upon, you're not ready to walk away. To fully enjoy the crewing lifestyle, you need to be free of problems hovering "back home."

You will not sell and sail immediately. It takes time to untangle your tangle, to liquidate your material possessions, to get your life pared down to the bare necessities. These activities are also good preparation and practice for living on a sailboat.

Continue working if you are currently employed and carefully plan your escape. There are bills to be paid, checking and savings accounts to be set up, your car to be sold, and your lifestyle to be changed.

I untangled in the following order: sold or gave away every last item in my house that would not fit into my planned sailing life; found a room to rent in a friend's house; sold my house; invested the profits; organized my traveling paperwork; quit my job; sold my car; packed my seabag; called a taxi; settled into the airplane seat. . . .

Living space and job decisions aside, there is more to consider: Get used to eating simple foods, salads, fresh fruits, and vegetables. While cooking and eating on a sailboat does not by any means mean a spartan existence, pizza and fried chicken are rarely available.

Turn off the television. Quit cold turkey and discover reading and music for entertainment. Store your jewelry and enjoy unadorned skin that the sun can reach. Toss out the makeup. If you cannot part with your material possessions and break your addictions, then maybe the sailing life is not for you.

As you gear down on land-bound dwelling and gear up for sailing, you will no longer need to shop. Outstanding bills get paid off fast! The major expenses you work to support on land are rent/mortgage, clothing, household decoration and maintenance, car insurance and repairs, entertainment, and a full share of grocery bills. You will not have these expenses while sailing.

So untangle your tangle. Don't rush it—take as long as you sensibly need, but work solidly toward your goal to eliminate all the landlubber expenses.

After you have simplified your living arrangements and

modified your lifestyle from landlocked to sailing, you should collect the paperwork you will need in order to travel. So, the next step is *Getting Your Ducks in a Row*.

2
Getting Your Ducks in a Row

Passport

It's best to make a personal trip to your post office or passport office. No matter what you hear, you probably won't be able to apply for or renew your passport, or make a change to it, in two weeks through the mail. Plan a personal visit and be patient!

Visas

Do not apply for any visas unless your captain asks you to. However, do not leave home assuming you will not need to know where they are needed and how to obtain one. I have never used a visa because the longest I've ever stayed in one port was one month in Greece.

Getting the list of countries requiring visas is easy. Everything you ever wanted to know about visas can be obtained by sending fifty cents and a stamped, self-addressed, business-size envelope to:

Consumer Information Center
P. O. Box 438T
Pueblo, Colorado 81009

Ask for a booklet entitled *Foreign Entry Requirements*.

Visas can be obtained from overseas embassies once you've determined you need one or have been asked to secure one. You can apply directly to the embassy (the embassy has application forms) of the country in which you wish to extend your stay.

Also available is a *Passport Survival Kit*, a "3-binder set which includes 500 pages of information on procedures and application forms for over 100 countries." If you are looking for a full circumnavigation you may need it. Write to:

Visa Advisors
1930 18th Street, NW
Washington, D.C. 20009
(202) 797-7976

Usually, when you're just passing through the more popular touristy countries on an oceangoing vessel, visas are not required. Keep in mind that visa requirements do change from time to time, so if in doubt ask your captain. After all, you never know where in the world you might sail, and being prepared is better than being left behind.

International Driver's License

An international driver's license can be obtained by taking two passport-style photos, your driver's license, and a small fee ($8.00) to your local American Automobile Association office. Or for ten dollars AAA will take your picture right at their facility. They issue an international driver's license on the spot and you do not have to be a member of AAA to obtain one. Even if you're not planning to drive in foreign countries, it's a good idea to carry it for extra identification.

Before you decide to rent any vehicle in a foreign country, make two attempts to cross any street in that country on foot. If you are successful on either of the two attempts, you might actually survive as a rental driver. There are no driving tests to take before renting; however, if you are expert at driving in reverse down a one-way street, making a U-turn from the extreme right- or left-hand lanes across oncoming traffic, and if you can manage keeping at least two wheels on the sidewalk for about a quarter mile, then rent something and go for it!

Inoculations and Health Record

State and local health departments can provide information on what shots to get. Call them. Let them know you will be traveling throughout the world but as yet do not know where, and ask them for the list of inoculations required. These may include cholera, typhoid, gamma globulin, yellow fever, tetanus, polio and others.

Most inoculations can be obtained from your local physician with the possible exception of yellow fever. Your State or local health department can give you locations in your area that supply the yellow fever vaccine.

Start your inoculations two months before you are ready to travel. A typhoid vaccination takes two shots a few weeks apart. Consult your physician for the proper inoculations for you, how long each inoculation protects you, and which require periodic boosters. Really, they don't hurt a bit. . . .

Remember to carry your inoculation record card with you as you travel.

IMPORTANT NOTE

Make a clear photocopy of your passport, driver's license, and inoculation record. Keep them together in an envelope and leave them in a safe deposit box or with someone dependable back home before you travel.

Mail

Since you will sell your mailing address if you sell your house, get permission to use a family member's or friend's mailing address in the States. Remind them that they will be responsible for packaging your mail (*sans* junk flyers) and sending it to you periodically during your travels.

Friends and other important people can reach you through that address while you are traveling. Be sure to call your mail-forwarder with the correct address in the area you're visiting. Or, as you travel, give clear, complete addresses where you can be reached in foreign ports each time you mail a letter out (see Chapter 10).

In the Mediterranean I didn't find American Express offices conveniently located for mail pick-up. They are more convenient to sailors in the Caribbean; however, there are other independent mail pick-up stations that are just as reliable (see list, Chapter 10).

Credit Card Bills

If you don't have a hometown resource for bill-paying, try leaving an appropriate sum of money on account with the credit card company whose card you will use while traveling. Leaving money on account and charging against it will cut down a little on the interest you would earn if your money sat in your savings account, but it also leaves you free to travel while meeting your charge card obligations. If you have sold everything and paid off your bills before traveling, you will not have regular bills other than perhaps an occasional charge for hotel or air fare while you are traveling.

Use only one credit card, if possible. VISA, MasterCard and American Express are accepted alternately throughout the world where tourists gather. An American Express card will *not* enable you to charge your traveler's check purchases either at their offices or any bank. You can do pretty much everything you need to do with a less expensive credit card like VISA or MasterCard.

Checking Account

If possible, set up a joint account with a family member back home—preferably the same responsible family member who is your mail collection point. Then you can have your credit card bills sent to that person, who can pay the bills out of your checking account in your absence and send you money should you need it while you travel.

In any case, carry your personal checkbook while traveling so you can buy traveler's checks and, if necessary, pay credit card bills.

Traveler's Checks

Purchase a minimum of $2000 in small-denomination traveler's checks before you leave. They're not easy to get in a hurry around the world. If you need to get additional traveler's checks in foreign ports, use a personal check to buy them from a bank, and be prepared to wait. You can speed the process by paying extra for the bank to telex, phone, or fax for approval. Otherwise, you might have to wait up to one week for your money in some areas of the world. Plan ahead and don't spend down to your last dollar before buying more. Use a worldwide major banking institution, such as Barclay's or Lloyds, as opposed to a smaller local bank.

As you sail from country to country, charge what you can (hotels, rental cars, air fare, restaurants), use personal checks where accepted, and save your "liquid cash" (traveler's checks) for the things you cannot obtain by credit card or personal check. You will need liquid cash for miscellaneous smaller purchases and services (see Chapter 4).

A Will

Most people don't like to acknowledge death and many avoid having a will prepared. Sailing is no more dangerous than driving on the crowded freeways and highways, or flying from one destination to the other. In most cases, it is safer. But be sensible and be prepared. Since anything can happen, anywhere in the world, be sure you have your bequests in order before you take off.

Knowledge and Skills

Sailing is fun, but it is also work. If you own your own boat, you'll be looking for crewmembers who can contribute to the safety of the passage, to the cleanliness of the boat, to the morale of the rest of the crew, and to the happiness of the outcome of the passage.

If you are traveling as a crewmember, you will want to make sure you have a skill to trade for passage on someone else's boat. So go into the world of sun and sea with some basic skills and knowledge, and be prepared to roll up your sleeves and contribute. (See Chapters 6 & 8).

Cooking is always a good skill to have (see Chapter 7), as is knowing how to swab a deck, splice a line, and follow orders smoothly. Take some sailing lessons, if possible; learn your knots, and learn to mend sails and lines if you can, but those skills are not necessarily required.

And how about learning some basic terminology? If you're acting as host/hostess on a sailboat, you may never need to know a winch from a wench. But, you should know that you work belowdecks (not downstairs) and that your main responsibility is the galley (not the kitchen). Bilges are any spaces underneath the cabin sole (not floor), and you will most likely be asked to scrub them out once in a while. Sailboats have heads (not bathrooms) and cabins and bunks (not bedrooms and beds). The pointed part of the boat is usually the bow (not the front). The tail end is called the stern; it's sometimes pointed as well (as on a double-ender), but as long as it follows behind the bow, it still remains the stern (not the back).

The left side as you face the bow is called the port side, and the right is the starboard side. Ropes are referred to as lines or halyards or sheets, depending upon their job, and the sails, miraculously, are simply called sails—until they're out of the bag and flying in position, at which point they go by their individual names—genoa, working jib, stays'l, main, reaching chute, mizzen, storm trys'l, drifter—and so on. Whew! Pick up a book on basic sailing and read it before you leave home.

When I sailed with a French captain, I asked him to teach me the terms he might call out in the heat of the moment, such as a spinnaker take-down, or a reefing operation. I committed to memory six or seven words and phrases in French. Later, when the wind came up, we had to drop the spinnaker, and the captain began calling out several unfamiliar phrases and words. I stood rooted to the spot, useless, while the captain expertly dashed around the boat and did all the necessary work himself. Later, I learned that he preferred to do most of the sail tuning and rapid changes by himself, which is why he taught us all the wrong words.

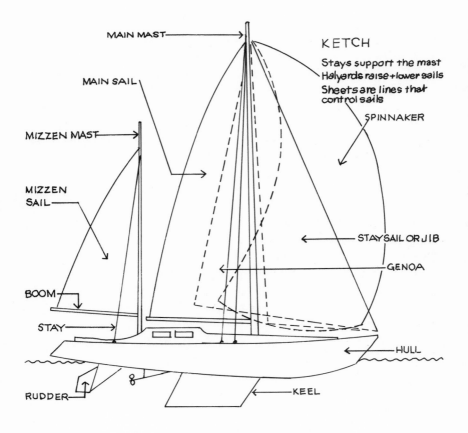

KETCH

Stays support the mast
Halyards raise + lower sails
Sheets are lines that control sails

MAIN MAST
MAIN SAIL
MIZZEN MAST
MIZZEN SAIL
BOOM
STAY
RUDDER
SPINNAKER
STAY SAIL OR JIB
GENOA
HULL
KEEL

If you have familiarized yourself with basic sailing terminology, you won't feel as though you have landed on a strange planet when the captain and crew sling around words like "abaft the beam" and "foc'sle."

If you can also learn the basics of repairing engines, or refrigeration, or marine heads, and understand the concept of navigation, it will help you find a berth, but it's not at all required before you leave. Don't let any of this "nice to have" information scare you off.

Some captains don't care if you have any sailing experience, wishing to teach you from scratch their way of doing things, including standing watch alone at night. Don't panic if you don't know a halyard from a winch, but a little preparation is suggested to make your crewing experience more enjoyable. And, for your own comfort and safety, be sure you're not prone to debilitating seasickness. Seasickness prevention patches, worn behind the ear, are available by prescription and work quite well.

When you travel to foreign countries, remember that you may leave the people who live there with a lasting impression of your home country. Make sure it's an impression that you and the rest of us can be proud of. You may even get invited back because of some kind deed you have done. Pick up trash. Do not leave any of your own. Do not be "ugly" and demanding.

Learn as much as you can about the customs and the language before you set foot on shore. Ask your captain about the accepted standards in each port you visit. Also, each sailing vessel on which you travel usually has a cruising guidebook which contains an overview of the customs and people of the area to be explored. Sailing gives you plenty of time to read.

Now you've untangled your tangle and gotten your ducks in a row. Next, you need to pack your seabag. While packing please remember, *Luggage Bearers Won't Be Needed.*

3

Luggage Bearers Won't Be Needed

No matter what areas of the oceans you plan to sail, hot or cold, leave the 20-piece, matched, designer suitcases at home.

IMPORTANT NOTE

Do not pack or carry more than you can comfortably handle alone. When you move from land to boats and walk long airport concourses, help with luggage is rarely available.

The Seabag

Most important is the type of luggage you will take: fabric and foldable. NO SUITCASES! Choose a sturdy, not cheap, seabag that is easy to handle, either to be slung over your shoulder or carried by strap-type handles. The easiest one to lock up is one that has not only carry handles but an overshoulder strap from end to end. A small lock can secure the zipper pull to the ring that holds the shoulder strap.

Any good marine products store will have a good selection of sturdy seabags. Before you determine the size of your seabag, collect all the items to be packed, measure the pile, then purchase the correct size bag to fit it all in comfortably. Your seabag will be filled with starter clothing and sundries as suggested in this chapter. In addition, keep a smaller, soft canvas airline-style carry-on to hold the miscellaneous items listed.

Sundries:

○ Good non-greasy skin creams and tanning lotions are a must! The sun's rays are concentrated on the water and reflection from the water's surface or boat deck will help burn even suntanned skin twice as fast, especially down around the southern latitudes (the world's and yours!).

○ When buying sunglasses, choose a pair that specifies UV protection. While Vuarnet® glasses are especially designed for the need of people on the water, there are other less expensive brands with good UV protection as well.

○ A soft canvas or cotton terry hat is a must. It preserves body fluids that the sun will steal quickly, and stows away nicely in your seabag.

What to Pack

This chapter contains lists of the essentials to pack and the special applications for certain items. Adapt this basic list to your personal preferences. Remember to buy fabrics that are lightweight and fast-drying.

Despite the prevalence of more stylish leather deck shoes, the ideal shoes are cheap canvas slip-ons with white (not black or colored) rubber soles. Clothing and shoes will get wet one way or another and bake dry in the sun between each dousing. Leathers harden and crack. Heavy materials stay damp and get moldy. Think cheap and disposable!

Instead of carrying a full set of foul-weather gear when you first start out, sail for a while to determine where you want to spend most of your time; determine whether or not it is needed, ask questions about the best type to purchase, and then buy it just before you need to use it. Carry lightweight rain gear for starters.

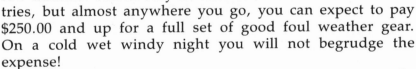

Before making an Atlantic crossing, you might want to purchase a good set of quality bib-type overalls, jacket and boots. By buying them right before they are needed, you will avoid carrying them around for a few months. Prices vary in different countries, but almost anywhere you go, you can expect to pay $250.00 and up for a full set of good foul weather gear. On a cold wet windy night you will not begrudge the expense!

I sailed from Greece to Gibraltar using only lightweight rubber rain gear to keep the larger waves off my dry clothing. The weather was suitably warm. When I arrived in Gibraltar, before crossing the Atlantic, I purchased a full set of Douglas Gill foul weather gear and boots, which I had the occasion to use during two unexpected storms. Had I used them only once, however, it would have been money well spent.

Whether your makeup is water soluble or not, don't bother using it. Very few people wear any kind of makeup at all on a sailboat because it is too impractical. If your makeup takes a lot of water to wash away, you will not always have an abundance of water available. Makeup rubs off on pillows and sheets, and laundries are not that readily available around the world. Carry the minimum if you wish to use it when not actively sailing or when "dressing up" for dinner in the evenings on land.

Basic Clothing

- three pair of lightweight shorts
- three tee shirts
- two pair of lightweight cotton slacks (drawstring or slip-ons are okay; men must always wear long pants in restaurants)
- two long-sleeve cotton tailored shirts (oversized to use as sun and mosquito protection)
- one casual dress (a sundress or slip-on tee-shirt material style looks fine with casual shoes)
- three pair of underthings (one to wear while the other is drying out, and a third just in case the second pair missed a rinsing and drying)
- two pareus (island-style lightweight rectangles of material that can be tied in many different ways)
- two swimsuits or bikinis
- two pair canvas slip-on white-soled shoes
- one pair rubber flip-flop shoes
- one pair thermal socks
- one pair thermal long-john underwear (Capilene® is excellent)
- one acrylic/polyester, zip front, elastic cuff and trim, windproof, perhaps waterproof, jacket
- sweatshirt

You will find as you work on a sailboat that your clothing will be destroyed fairly quickly one way or another. You will find things to snag on, places where you would never expect grease to be, and laundry services turning your once-good clothing into rags. Keep one tee shirt and pair of shorts for the dirty work on the sailboat and the rest for wearing on land or looking nice on board.

In the warmer climates, while not working on the boat, you can wear swimwear with a pareu cover-up (where a cover-up is necessary) and go barefoot on deck. Men wear either swim trunks or shorts only. To scrub bilges and decks wear your "work" outfit (the tee-shirt and shorts you get permanent grease stains on first). On land, wear either shorts and a tee shirt or long-sleeved shirts and pants as local custom dictates. For dinners in nice restaurants you can usually wear casual attire, and the pants or sun dress with canvas deck shoes work fine.

Do not think because you are heading for warmer latitudes that you will not get cold. You may hit a night or two when the thermal socks and jacket will come in handy. Better to go prepared.

Canvas shoes are ideal for strolling around the land. You might also want to pack a sturdy (but light) pair of walking shoes or running shoes. These are for longer walks around an island or rugged hiking if you are so inclined. Flip-flops are handy to wear in showers for preventing picking up foot diseases. Rubber sandals are ideal for wearing while you swim. Dangerous stonefish and poisonous corals are unfortunate hazards in some areas and wearing shoes in the water is recommended.

Remember to remove any shoes before
stepping onto a deck.

As you travel to different places you will find that you will add (conservatively) to your sailing wardrobe. Keep in mind the finite space in your seabag. Replace items that self-destruct or die a natural death. Do not overpack!

Personal Products:
(adapt this to your personal needs):

- two toothbrushes
- one large tube of toothpaste
- one shampoo (biodegradable and for use in salt water, available at marine supply stores)
- one hair conditioner (constant sun is tough on hair)
- one deodorant (be kind to fellow crew)
- a bar of soap
- dental floss
- small battery powered razor (men & women)
- a small can of shaving cream
- one bottle of eyedrops
- one pair of tweezers (men, too, for splinters)
- cotton-tipped swabs (cleans salt water out of ears)
- toenail and fingernail clippers
- a pumice stone (feet get rough and calloused)
- a moisturizing body cream (non-greasy)
- a bottle or two of Avon Skin-So-Soft® (the most effective insect repellent, non-chemical. Mix half the oil with water and use sparingly, being careful not to get it on boat decks and fabrics) or
- rub-on insect repellent or citronella

First-Aid Kit:

- a handful of medium-sized plastic strips
- a tube of good antibacterial ointment

- a roll of gauze

- a roll of waterproof adhesive tape

- a tube of any effective anti-itch cream (for nasty insect bites)

- a package of antihistamine capsules (combats excessive itching and inflammation from bites)

- a package of decongestant cold capsules

- an over-the-counter bottle of pain relievers

- a bottle of all-purpose vitamins and minerals

Based on your medical history, your doctor might write prescriptions and give careful instructions for the use of the following to include in your first-aid kit. Be sure to keep the list of prescription drugs, signed by your doctor, to present to foreign country officials upon request:

- a ten-day series of penicillin pills

- medication to control severe diarrhea

- malaria pills and fever powder

- a small supply of prescription pain-killers for cases of extreme pain (impacted tooth, broken bones) when no medical help is near

- a 6-month supply of whatever medication you might already be taking on a regular basis

By explaining my uncertain sailing itinerary to my doctor, I was able to carry the above specialized medications. By being careful while I traveled, I never had to use any of them.

A special note regarding birth control pills: Ladies, if you take them, and you get seasick, your pill will not work. (It does stop the fish from getting pregnant.) So be careful! If you do not wish to become pregnant, use an alternate form of contraceptive while sailing if seasickness is a problem.

And that is about it—the basics—unless you want to add a few things you just cannot live without. You will not have a problem resupplying these items as you travel throughout the areas noted in this book. A waterproof pouch or two will hold all of these items comfortably and tuck into your seabag.

Miscellaneous:
(adapt to personal tastes)

- ○ sunglasses with UV protection

- ○ a waterproof, pocket-size cassette player and foldable travel earphones (for occasional use on long night watches, or to enjoy music without disturbing others)

- ○ a small assortment of your favorite tapes (include music to relax with, music to wake up your senses)

- ○ a notebook to record your adventures

- ○ air-mail writing tablet and air-mail envelopes

- ○ a mechanical pencil with leads and extra erasers

- ○ ball-point pen

- ○ prescription glasses and sunglasses (if necessary)

- ○ sunglass strings, attached to your glasses and hung around your neck

- ○ a travel clothesline and six or eight clothespins

- ○ a travel sewing kit

- ○ a small pair of scissors

- ○ a pocket knife with a variety of blades and corkscrew (pack in your seabag, not carry-on luggage)

○ a few pairs of soft foam earplugs (for airplanes, noisy hotel rooms or noisy nights on boats)

○ a waterproof watch with calendar and alarm

○ a flashlight

A special note here for the ladies: if you wear internal protection during your period, try o.b.® brand tampons, which are compact to carry and create fewer disposal problems.

Add anything that would make your trimmed-down-to-the-bare-necessities life more comfortable, but this is about all that will fit in your seabag and carry-on bag. No VCRs or tennis rackets or any electronics will be necessary. Towels and washcloths are provided in hotels and rooming houses and on boats. You still might want to carry a lightweight towel for sanitary reasons if you do not care to share towels.

Plug-in hair dryers, razors, and other electrical gadgets purchased in your home town will not work with foreign outlets and currents. Let the wind dry your hair and rediscover the fun the pioneers had before electricity. I looked forward each evening, after a hot, hard day of work on board, to taking a cool shower and brushing my wet hair out in the warm breezes wafting across the bow.

So you have untangled your tangle, gotten your ducks in a row, and packed your seabag. *Now You'll Need A Little Money.*

4

You'll Need a Little Money

Nothing is free. However, I discovered that this lifestyle can be beautifully inexpensive if you are not a shop-till-you-drop kind of person. Before you spend what you start with, you might even begin earning money if you choose charter boats as your crewing targets. More about that later.

For starters, you'll need at least $5,000 in an accessible bank account, preferably savings, from which you can withdraw or transfer funds easily when in foreign countries. This cushion provides peace of mind and gets you through any small emergencies. If possible, place an additional $1,000 in a personal or joint checking account. And take off with $2,000 in traveler's checks. That's a total starting fund of $8,000. You won't use much of that money if you are determined to sail.

As mentioned previously, you will also be carrying one major credit card. Traveler's checks will be used for smaller expenditures like bus fares, taxis, meals, local phone calls and personal items. If you will be making a fair amount of long-distance calls, use a telephone company calling card or call collect.

By now you're probably wondering how you can travel on so little. Well, the biggest expense you had on land while you dreamed of a simpler lifestyle stemmed not only from your mortgage/rent payments and car payments, but shopping for clothing, gadgets, food and things—lots of things to fill your house and car and office. You won't have those expenses any more. After all, how much can you fit in a seabag?

Besides, when you travel as a crewmember, you exchange labor for your meals on board and your bunk, thereby eliminating monthly rent or mortgage payments. You exchange reading material with other sailors, and possibly trade cassette tapes as well. You will only have infrequent hotel bills and some small grocery bills.

Being a crewmember on a larger charter boat is a paid position in most cases. Remember to keep records of your earnings for reporting tax according to the laws of your home state. You will not find much to spend your earnings on over and above your personal "consumable" items and a few articles of replacement clothing.

Living so much better for so much less sounds pretty good, but since life presents surprises every day, don't get overconfident and waste your money.

IMPORTANT NOTE

If you cannot afford to pay for a few days' hotel and meals on land in between crewing assignments, or the cost of a ticket home, *do not enter this lifestyle until you are financially ready.* It makes good sense not to be financially dependent upon anyone.

When you get on a crew list you become the financial responsibility of the captain, and a captain does not want to take on a burdensome crewmember. Some captains may want to see evidence of a ticket to your next destination, and some countries (Antigua, for one) require that you purchase such a ticket before entering. In fact, because I was the only prospective crewie with an airline ticket from Antigua to the U.S. Virgin Islands, I was accepted as crew in Bequia on a boat sailing to Antigua.

Should you need to purchase an airline ticket, buy a standard open-return ticket that is changeable and refundable unless you actually plan to return on a specific date. For instance, when I left California I purchased a round-trip ticket with an open return. When I reached Grenada, I traded in the return for a ticket that hopped up the island chain in the event I could not find a boat. That was the ticket that came in handy when I was accepted as crew in Bequia. Be sure to shop for the best air fares and deals to your destinations.

Now, keeping in mind moderate inflation, the following information includes ballpark expenses for each of the places mentioned in this book. These are average expenditures on land for rooms, food, transportation, medical and dental expenses, and miscellaneous needs.

Rooms

You will probably want to book your first night in an unfamiliar land in a moderately priced room. You will probably be tired from your first day in planes and airports, and by paying a bit more for a nicer room, you will have a shower, a comfortable bed, and a private place to collect your wits before you venture out into the boating lifestyle. You can get information on rooms in this price range before you arrive in a new area by calling the tourist bureau for that area.

From that home base you can venture out and find a boat, or private house with rooms to rent, a pension, or other less expensive accommodations closer to the harbor.

Give yourself three days to one week of land living while looking for your first boat. If you're determined enough to get your toes on a sunny deck, and if you've started in the right place at the right time (see Chapter 5) your search should not take too long.

The Mediterranean is affordable no matter where you go—Greece and Turkey, especially—but you will find prices rising gradually as you venture toward Italy, Spain, the Caribbean, and the U.S. In all references to the Mediterranean I am including from Turkey on the Aegean sea to Gibraltar for simplicity.

I found Rhodes, Greece the least expensive and most convenient area to live while looking for a boat. Pensions abound, as do private rooms, and inexpensive hotel rooms—all within a short walk of the harbor. And there are many boats in Mandraki Harbor to choose from.

In old Rhodes, right by the harbor, there are hundreds of rooms for rent, from a few dollars to twenty dollars per night. There the rooms are tucked away in ancient medieval buildings with narrow cobbled streets and iron-framed windows. You could not ask for a more picturesque surrounding—noisy (remember to pack earplugs), but unique.

Accommodations for travelers are well advertised, and almost anyone you ask can point you there. Some rooms have a toilet and shower, some have them down the hall on a shared basis. Be sure to ask. In many cases, you will find people right at the waterfront offering inexpensive accommodations and handing out their information to passers-by.

You will find as you sail from one country to the next that you will spend most of your time down by the harbor. That is where the cities are. That is where the yachties are. That is where the action is. Ask anyone for information about an inexpensive place to stay and you cannot go wrong.

At many marinas you can rent a spare cabin on a boat for $20.00 per night, or $100.00 a week. Some boats advertise on the marina bulletin boards, others by word of mouth. There is no shortage of helpful mouths offering information at any marina. Some boats are managed by yacht service agencies right on the dock. It is much safer for an individual staying alone to be on a boat in the anchorage than in the city. Besides, the marina is where you need to be, so it saves transportation costs.

Should you not have access to your boat's dinghy, a commercial or private water taxi is usually cruising around the anchorages looking for folks to ferry about. In Bequia and St. Thomas water taxis are very convenient and only fifty cents to a dollar fifty per ride. However, you can usually flag down a friendly sailor in a dinghy going your direction or stand on the dinghy dock and wait for someone to come along. It doesn't take long. No matter where, fellow sailors are a friendly, helpful lot.

Food

Depending upon your eating habits you may be buying one to three meals per day on land when you're not crewing on a boat. Depending upon the country you're in, you could pay from a few dollars to a hundred dollars per meal, again depending upon your choice of eating establishments. You can always find a good inexpensive meal.

From the Mediterranean to the Caribbean, you can find wholesome and plentiful meals of grilled fish, green salad, rice or fries, bread, barbecued chicken, or even octopus and squid for an average of seven dollars per meal. Many hearty meals are much less—three dollars to five dollars—depending on whether the main course is fish or chicken. Beef and lamb in the Mediterranean are reasonably priced, while fish is always more expensive.

A really good way to find the best-for-less meals any-where you travel is to avoid the obvious tourist places and ask a local where you can get a good home-cooked meal. There are lots of simple little establishments tucked away where locals eat. The food is never disappointing.

Even on the little island of Bequia, where you might think your choice of restaurants was limited and perhaps pricey, you will find a place for "chicken and chips" upstairs over a supermarket, without a sign proclaiming it as a restaurant. The locals know about it and will point the way when asked. It is, without a doubt, the best fried chicken you will ever eat—about three dollars for more than you can eat—packed with a delicious local spiced sauce.

You can even avoid restaurants by buying fresh fruits, bread, peanut butter, yogurt, milk, cheese, or whatever, at local markets. These can be stored easily in your room or purchased daily.

Transportation

You may need transportation during the day when you are on land. If you pick a hotel or rooming house near the harbor you can rely on your feet quite a bit. Just about every port has telephone, telex, bank, post office, taxi and bus service right down by the waterfront, and unless you want to sightsee, you probably will not need wheels. Rental cars and mopeds are also available, but unless you have nerves of steel and a death wish, do not drive in foreign countries.

BUSES   Bus fares are the least expensive, ranging from around sixty cents to two dollars per trip throughout the Mediterranean and Caribbean—but be prepared to be packed in like a sardine in a standing-room-only situation. This is definitely not recommended transportation for claustrophobics! Nevertheless, buses are usually the best transportation bargains. They run everywhere—sometimes right over the taxis—in their enthusiasm to get you where you need to go.

TAXIS   Taxi fares throughout the Mediterranean are around two dollars to five dollars, depending upon the distance you wish to travel. Short hops through the city of Rhodes usually range from around a dollar fifty cents to two dollars. Be sure to negotiate the fare and agree with the driver before you get in the taxi. Some drivers work on an independent pricing scale based on whether or not you look like a rich tourist.

In Gibraltar, Seville, and Madeira, you can walk from the harbor or marina to just about anywhere unless you wish to do long-distance sightseeing. Sightseeing rates for buses and taxis are posted in local information brochures available at marina offices or conveniently located tourist information offices in town.

Coming from the Mediterranean to the Caribbean you'll notice everything getting more expensive—around five to ten dollars per ride down in the Grenadines, and rising slightly higher the farther up the chain you travel. Twenty dollars in Antigua (the Caribbean) will get you from English Harbour to the airport roughly fifteen miles away. In contrast, a much longer taxi ride, from one side of Mykonos (the Mediterranean) to the other, costs only seven dollars. Buses are always less expensive. But you can see more and meet more people as you pass the shops and sidewalk vendors on foot.

CARS AND MOPEDS   In the Mediterranean, and the Caribbean, including the Windward and Leeward islands, you can rent a car (which you will drive on the left side of the road in many countries) for an average of $35.00 per day plus "petrol" ($2.00 per liter and up, depending upon area and current world oil situation). Bargains are always available if you call around and compare. Ask for the smallest car available and be sure to ask if the price includes free mileage.

Remember to ask about a Collision Damage Waiver. This is optional, but recommended. With CDW you are fully covered for *everything* (read the fine print on all insurance forms).

For the most part, you will be surprised at how close and accessible everything is; you don't really need wheels to see and do a lot, not only in the Mediterranean but in the Caribbean as well. You do not get much exercise on a sailboat no matter what your duties, so let your hair go free, dress in lightweight shorts and shirt, a comfortable pair of walking shoes, and let your feet show you the wonders of each area you visit.

Medical/Dental

Unless you have an ongoing illness that needs follow-up medical attention, you won't need to carry medical insurance for your travels. First, you should be in good health to take on a journey of this sort. Second, convenient doctors and dentists are not always in abundance once you leave your home town.

It's best to be "self-insured" and prepared to pay cash for your medical/dental needs as you travel. These expenses can be covered by credit card, traveler's check, or personal check (where accepted). Then, by contacting your savings bank back home, you can transfer the necessary funds into your checking account for eventual replacement of traveler's checks.

See a dentist before you leave home. Have necessary fillings done, crowns installed where needed, etc. Dentists are not available in the middle of the ocean, or on remote islands, or in deserted anchorages. Be prepared.

I suggest self-insurance and preventive dental care because I found many home-town insurers will not cover you for a journey of this type. Should you find one, by the time you have paid the premiums, and the deductible, you can just as well have paid the bills yourself. Keep at least a thousand dollars of the initial five thousand in your starting account earmarked for medical expenses, though you should never have to use all of that. If you work carefully around sailboat equipment and take normal health precautions as you travel, you shouldn't need to be too concerned with medical bills. It is prudent though to keep your basic hospital coverage in case something really bad happens to you.

Miscellaneous

Your expense on land might also include postage and telephone calls. Postage is pretty reasonable into the U.S. as well as to other European countries from the Mediterranean or the Caribbean. Letters go by weight and size, and you might pay as much as a dollar for a real whopper. Other than that, thirty to seventy five cents per letter was the rate to the U.S., depending upon country of origin. Try to avoid mailing large packages, because then the price goes sky high. (And it's not too easy to find a decent box.)

Buying stamps in a foreign country can sometimes be an adventure in itself. In Rhodes I asked for five stamps and was handed ten. I smiled and repeated that I only needed five. The teller, named Maria, began a five-minute argument in Greek with the teller next to her (also named Maria), then continued to insist that I needed ten stamps. Having purchased stamps there before, I knew what I needed, and persisted in my request for only five stamps. By then, the first Maria was scowling, convinced that all Americans were troublemakers. She gave me four stamps. I knew when to compromise. I took my four stamps, scowled right back, and went to the corner newspaper stand to buy one more.

A special note about mailing things home to family and friends: If you find a cardboard box in the tropics or elsewhere and use it to mail goods home, remind the receiver to discard the box outside immediately after unpacking it. Cardboard boxes house cockroach eggs (see Chapter 6).

Telephone calls to local numbers are not expensive no matter where you are. It's best to make all calls from the local telephone company or pay phone and *not* from your hotel or rooming house (which often charge more than the phone company), unless you are using a pay-as-you-go telephone. Local calls range from twenty to fifty cents per call throughout the Mediterranean and the Caribbean; long-distance calls, however, can end up costing you an arm and a leg, so keep them short. They are charged on a per-minute basis and three dollars per minute is a good (excessive, but good) rule of thumb. Use your calling card, or call collect.

That's about it for costs on land and while you are crewing. Not so bad, really, if you watch your spending. During my one-month stay in Rhodes' Mandraki Harbor I spent (not because I had to, but because I had not learned controlled spending yet) perhaps $500.00, primarily on new foods I had never eaten, phone calls home, and postage—and then earned almost $300.00 working on another boat in port while the one on which I was to crew was in dry dock.

Currency Exchange

When you exchange the currency you carry for the locally accepted currency, do so at a bank where you will get the highest exchange rate and be charged the lowest commission for the transaction. Exchange rates seem to vary on a daily basis in every country, and ten dollars exchanged on Tuesday may buy more or less local currency than on Wednesday. Avoid exchanging money at bars, hotels, or supermarkets where you will lose more money in the exchange than you would care to. Use their services only in an emergency, and then exchange only the amount you will need to complete that one transaction.

Banks accept only paper money, never coins, of other countries. And in some places, even paper money of another country is not accepted. Private businesses do not accept currency or coins from other countries. Ask in each bank, before you exchange your money, where the local currency is and is not accepted once you leave that country. Ask at a few different banks, if possible, because answers will vary from clerk to clerk.

Exchange money in small amounts, in the country in which you will use it, to ensure you spend it before you exchange more. At times your captain's plans might change overnight, and you could be leaving a country faster than you expected.

Should you earn money in a foreign country as a paid crewmember, you would do best to spend the money in the country where you earned it. It's next to impossible to exchange local currency back to U.S. dollars, even at a bank. For example, the maximum amount of U.S. dollars you can obtain in exchange for drachmas in Greece is $100.00. You must provide a passport and fill out lots of forms and wade through lots of red tape and . . . spend the drachmas, have fun.

You may find that, because you can usually buy more of "their" money with less of yours, things cost "less" compared to what they would cost at home. But everything is relative. Do not fall back into old shopping habits, thinking you are getting a bargain, and buy things you don't need.

You have, thus far, untangled your tangle, gotten your ducks in a row, packed your seabag and obtained a little money. Now you have to find *Where the Boats Float*.

5

Where the Boats Float

Now we get to the nitty gritty. You're ready to go and you need a place to start. Well, you certainly have a lot of places from which to choose, depending upon the time of year you're ready to start sailing. This chapter covers *where* to find the boats and *when*; but first, you should know *how*.

How to Find a Crewing Position

After you land at the airport, take a taxi to your rented room, then ask directions to the yacht harbor. Use your feet or inexpensive ground transportation to get there. Find your crewing positions by walking the docks at the marinas, posting notices, registering with crewfinding agencies and frequenting yachtie hangouts. Keep your eyes and ears open. Ask lots of questions and don't be shy. Like any other good job you're determined to get, you literally have to "pound the pavement."

At the pleasure craft marinas and yacht harbors, ask people standing on a deck if they need crew for their boat. If they don't need anyone, they may know of someone who does. Go to the yachtie hangouts and relax with a cold drink. Tell everyone wearing deck shoes that you're looking for a crewing position. Tell the bartenders and waitresses where the yachties gather to drink and eat, too. Read the crew notices posted on the bulletin boards and at the marina offices and markets where yachties buy their provisions. While this book gives specific names and locations, it is your enthusiasm and determination that will get you on a boat. You won't believe how easy it is until you get there.

Many boats carry a crew of mixed nationality. If you plan to start your travels in a foreign country, try learning the basics of other languages, or start with the boats flying flags of countries whose languages you already know.

My first try for a crewing position began in Mandraki Harbor. I took a long walk down the quay, surveying the hundreds of boats, noting flags from at least ten countries, and watching the activity. Then I approached a boat flying an Australian flag and asked the first person I saw on deck, "Do you need crew?" Within three hours (mostly waiting for a referred boat to return) I had my first crewing assignment—cruising the south coast of Turkey in exchange for labor—on a lovely 47-foot French sailing vessel. The captain was delightful, and even took the time to teach me some of his beautiful language.

About posting notices: On a full sheet of paper or an index-card, try this:

> CREWING POSITION WANTED—(long or short passage—state preference). Available (immediately, or give date). Special skills (list whatever applies, such as cook, bilge-scrubber and general deckhand, marine mechanic, experienced first mate, enthusiastic beginner willing to learn all jobs). (State whether you are a smoker or non-smoker.)

Print all information clearly, give first name only, contact number or place of residence, best time to be reached, etc.

Be clean, trim and presentable at all times. If you look like you cannot take care of yourself, you will most likely not be entrusted with someone's boat.

If you are timid you will not find a boat. You need to plunge right in to make your dream a reality. If you don't ask that first question, you'll be left standing on the dock watching opportunities pulling in and out at the rate of one per minute. Follow up on the information you get and you will soon have a deck under your feet.

Post notices in marine supply stores, sailmakers' lofts, yacht brokerages, yacht grocery supply stores, and marina offices (where allowed). Where the boats float, crews are always needed. No matter where you start your search, the more you spread your name around, the more successful your search will be.

Where and When to Find the Boats

Now that you know how to find the sailboats and the jobs, you'll need to know specifically *where* and *when*. This is, of course, the key to sailing. Sailors and their boats follow the seasons and stay well away from hurricanes and other life-threatening weather. Once you start sailing, chances are you will live in perpetual spring and summer conditions if you so choose. So sling your seabag over your shoulder and pick your starting point.

Start with your nearest-to-home pleasure boat marinas. Stroll the docks, read the posting boards, scan the ads in marine publications, ask questions in sailmaker shops and marine supply stores. People planning a long voyage will most likely stock up on sails and spare parts before they depart.

West Coast of the United States

Boats start heading south from northern climates around the end of the summer through the middle of October.

In Washington State there are a few good hunting grounds, but make note that most serious long-distance cruisers will be gone by October. So, start your search late spring and through the summer.

One highly recommended place is Point Hudson Harbor in Port Townsend. Drop in at Port Townsend Sails, post a notice and chat with the customers. Another excellent source of information on long-distance cruisers is Schattauer Sails on

Seaview Avenue, N.W., in Seattle. Schattauer Sails is near Shilshole Marina.

Or, hang out in Neah Bay, west of Port Angeles, which is the last jumping-off place before Cape Flattery. Inexpensive accommodations can be found while you are looking for passage south.

If you are in Seattle during January and February, you might want to sit in on one of the monthly meetings of the Puget Sound Cruising Club. They meet once a month at the North Seattle Community College. Call the college for meeting dates.

San Francisco and Sausalito are two more areas of potential. Check in with the Island Yacht Club in Alameda for information on long-distance cruisers. Or walk through the Sanford-Wood Boatyard on Cutting Boulevard across the Bay in Richmond. There are many public docks in Sausalito across the Golden Gate bridge from San Francisco. For instance, there's the Sausalito Yacht Harbor right in the center of Sausalito. Or the Pelican Yacht Harbor adjacent to the Sausalito Yacht Harbor.

You can also post a notice on the bulletin board at West Marine on Harbor Drive in Sausalito. Once you start your search, information will flow and you'll discover all the other good spots in that area.

If you prefer to start your search in a warmer climate during September, October and November, there are some excellent hunting grounds in San Diego, California. Many cruising vessels coming down from Canada and the northern regions of the West Coast stop in San Diego for fuel, parts, reprovisioning, and rest before continuing their journey to either Mexico, Hawaii, or the South Pacific islands. Cruising vessels also take on crew in San Diego for these long passages.

The following organizations sponsor a once-a-year party, open to the general sailing public, around the end of October or early November. These parties provide a common gathering place for yachties and prospective crew to match up in a relaxed, informal atmosphere.

Kona Kai International Yacht Club
1551 Shelter Island Drive
San Diego, CA 92106
(619) 223-3138

The Kona Kai is located at the Port of Entry to San Diego next to the Customs' dock. Dock privileges are available to guests from reciprocating yacht clubs. The Kona Kai hosts a party of several hundred people early in November. In addition to the opportunity to mix and mingle with captains and crew alike, you also gain access to a data base specifically compiled to match crew with boats. You need only register at the party.

Pacific Marine Supply
2804 Canon Street
San Diego, CA 92106
(619) 223-7194

Yachts check in for parts and supplies at the Pacific Marine Supply. It not only hosts a big cruising kickoff party (end of October/early November), but also offers a VHF network for matching crew to yachts, and a crew-posting bulletin board.

Downwind Marine
2819 Canon Street
San Diego, CA 92106
(619) 224-2733

Downwind Marine caters to cruising yachts, holds a cruising party around the same time, offers a meeting place for captains and crew, and a crew-posting bulletin board. The owner, Chris Frost, extends a friendly welcome to sailing enthusiasts.

You may also want to spend some time at the Police Dock at the end of Shelter Island. There are twenty-five slips set aside for cruising vessels down from northern climes on their way to points farther south and across the Pacific.

Two publications targeting the sailing crowd, "Latitude 38" and "Santana", can be found at any of these organizations and in the local marinas. They contain crew lists and advertisements and are yet another resource for matching crew to captains. As in all public advertising, however, "let the buyer beware."

East Coast of the United States

From Maine to the abundant boat-hunting grounds of Florida, the best time to begin your search is November, December or January. Head for the marinas up along the eastern coastline if you can handle the cold weather while you look. There's a good migration of East Coast sailors who flee the snow and cold winds from the Carolinas north, to winter in southern Florida, the Bahamas, or the Florida Keys. Others will make the passage to the Virgin Islands and cruise there for the season, which runs from December through the first of May, and then sail home for the spring thaw.

Boats planning to circumnavigate the globe will prepare for the trip and then leave from the southern reaches of Florida around the end of February, heading toward the Panama Canal. To sail with good weather, boats need to be through the Canal by then if they're heading for the South Pacific.

There are crewfinding agencies in Florida where you can register your name, skills, and type of trip you would like. These agencies put crews and boats together for a reasonable fee. Because there are so many marinas and places where boats gather in Florida, they just might make your search a short one:

> Crewfinders International, Inc.
> 404 S.E. 17th Street
> Ft. Lauderdale, FL 33316
> (305) 522-2739

Crew Unlimited
2065 South Federal Highway
Ft. Lauderdale, FL 33316
(305) 462-4624

Captains and Crew
1342 S.E. 17th Street
Ft. Lauderdale, Fl 33316
(305) 524-2739

The Caribbean

Boats start arriving like flocks of homing pigeons to the Caribbean around the middle to end of December. The Canary Islands sponsor a race each year, the ARC, which takes off from Las Palmas, Gran Canaria around November 24 and ends in Barbados throughout December. While the end point may change, beginning is always the Canary Islands and the date holds steady around November 24th.

This "race" is a fun way for migrating charter boats of all types and sizes to have company on the Atlantic crossing. Crew is always needed and you need not know a thing about racing to participate.

Once you arrive in the Caribbean, plan to settle in, either on a boat or on land, for the two-week Christmas/New Year holiday season. Not many boats sail then, but everyone parties. So kick back and relax, attend a weekly barbecue and jump-up, enjoy the steel bands, and absorb the local culture.

After the holidays, the cruising season in the Caribbean runs from approximately the beginning of December through the end of April or early May. Then captains organize their crews for the return crossing back to the Mediterranean, up to the United Kingdom, or the United States.

There are so many excellent places to sign on as crew, it's hard to include them all. Listed are some prime hunting grounds, which will give you a few good places to start. Once you're there and talking to fellow sailors, you'll get lots of other ideas.

VIRGIN ISLANDS Without a doubt, Yacht Haven Marina in Charlotte Amalie, the main harbor on St. Thomas, is the place to be. Not only do you have ample docks to walk, you also have the Bridge Bar and Grill upstairs overlooking the action. From five p.m. to seven p.m. you can have a drink, swap stories, and find crewing assignments in an open-air bar/restaurant happy hour.

In addition, there are agencies right there in the marina that put boats and crew together. Sometimes the agencies' names change, sometimes their offices move, but they all remain right there at the marina complex. First there's Regency Charter Services, located in the hot pink building at the top of the steps leading down into the marina. Regency prefers that you provide them with a resume and photo for their files (P.O. Box 9997, St. Thomas, USVI 00801 (809) 776-5300). Then there's Flagship Services, across the road from Regency and down the path, with a bulletin board for general crew postings. They provide placements, however, primarily for professional captains and cooks. If you are a captain or cook, provide this agency with a resume, which they will keep on file for boat owners to peruse. Finally, Captains and Crew has a Virgin Islands branch located directly under The Bridge restaurant near the gas dock.

In addition to the crewfinding agencies there is a large bulletin board in plain view on the wall over the steps leading down to the marina. With all of these placement services, nightly happy hour in The Bridge, hundreds of boats in and out daily, and highly visible posting boards, you cannot help but find a crewing position right away.

When coming from one of the U.S. Virgin Islands into the British Virgin Islands you must check in with customs upon entering, so keep your passport handy. You will have no problem securing a crewing position in St. Thomas and cruising the BVIs. The Virgin Island chain offers some of the best cruising grounds and anchorages in the world.

BARBADOS   Finding plentiful crewing positions here depends largely on whether or not the ARC race ends here. There is only one dock in Bridgetown where the ARC racers come in as they complete their Atlantic crossing—the main dock at the commercial shipping port. You cannot miss it. Large tents are set up on the dock. Customs and immigration are there to check people in. Food and festivities are arranged there. The activity starts around the second week in December when the first boats begin arriving.

After the crossing, captains begin looking for cruising season crew (deckhands, hostesses, cooks, first mates); crew look for other boats on which to sail, depending upon their needs and skills; everyone parties for the holiday season all up and down the island chain; and no one really does any serious sailing during this time.

If you start your search in Barbados, do so at the commercial dock among the ARC racers. Or, hang out at The Boatyard bar (on the beach in town), which faces the small bay where hundreds of the cruising yachts anchor after they leave the commercial dock. There are no marinas or docking facilities in Barbados, so you'll need to make friends with someone with a dinghy.

Barbados is probably the most expensive area to spend time on land. Inexpensive accommodations are available by asking at the yachtie hangouts. However, it's best to secure a crewing position as soon as you arrive, and thereby minimize your expenses.

ANTIGUA   English Harbour is another excellent place around mid-December to secure a prime crewing position. Not only do some ARC participants head straight for this beautiful island after checking in at Barbados, but so do other private yachts and cruisers who have just completed the Atlantic crossing. There's a dock along which you can walk that also accommodates gigantic power vessels.

In addition, there are many yachtie hangouts within an arm's length of each other: The Galley Bar (where you can step off the front porch onto the dock), The Copper & Lumber Store, Abracadabra's, and Limey's, just to name a few. There is ample anchorage and many of the larger charter boats gather in beautiful English Harbour as home base for the charter season.

If strolling the dock or talking with yachties at the gathering places does not turn up your ideal crew position, check with Nicholson's, right in English Harbour. This yacht service company books charter vacations for many of the larger charter boats, and is most helpful and informative about boats in need of crew.

ST. LUCIA, BEQUIA, GRENADA, VENEZUELA It is important to keep in mind the Christmas and New Year holiday season. In spite of the warm weather, skies full of stars, and palms swaying in the warm evening tradewinds, it's still holiday season, when sailing activity virtually stops and partying is plentiful. If you're not crewing on a yacht by mid-December, you might have to plan to stay put on land somewhere until after the first of the year. Many boats found holidaying in these four beautiful locations will take on crew right after the first of the year to begin the cruising season.

In St. Lucia the most promising area to concentrate your search is Rodney Bay Marina. There's ample dock space, as well as anchoring grounds, and quite a few yachtie hangouts. The A Frame is the prime yachtie bar in Rodney Bay. Or try Jimmy's Place near the Port Castries Yacht Center. And don't miss the every-Friday-night street party and jump-up in Gros Islet. Follow the crowds cramming into the buses, or walking, and prepare to have a great time!

Take the ferry from Kingstown on St. Vincent to get to Bequia. There are two areas where the yachts gather in Bequia, and you can see both of them from the ferry dock. One anchorage is Lower Bay, where the holding ground is better for anchors. Da Reef and Sunny Caribbee yachtie hangouts are located in Lower Bay.

The main anchorage, Elizabeth Harbour, joins tail-to-nose with Lower Bay and has the heaviest concentration of boats, even though their anchors occasionally drag and boats bounce off each other. The boats gather primarily in this area because of The Frangipani, The Green Boley, The Whale Boner, Mack's Pizza, and The Clubhouse. All of these are yachtie hangouts, in a row, on a footpath that runs along the water's edge.

Across little Elizabeth Harbour there's the Harpoon Saloon and the gas dock, where all boats eventually go for water and fuel. You can post notices in both places, as well as in the Frangipani Yacht Office. There are also marine supply stores, yacht grocery supply stores, the post office, the customs and immigration office, and a tourist information kiosk right there along the water's edge in town.

For a sleeping place on land, there's a small guest house down by the main anchoring ground. The guest house is owned and operated by Lyston at The Green Boley. Drop in at The Green Boley and have a chat with Lyston about his rock-bottom room rates, and don't forget to order a rum punch or lime slush.

In Grenada there are only a few really good places to look for boats, and a stay on land can get expensive if you want to live down by the water. First, there's the town of St. George's, the main harbor area where the cruise ships dock, but where sailboats can only anchor out. The main hangout is The Nutmeg, an upstairs bar/restaurant overlooking the anchorage— the best place to concentrate your search.

There's a docking facility around the coast in another bay for sailboats, Grenada Yacht Services, but the dock itself is in sad shape since the "intervention" some years ago, and may no longer be functional by the time you arrive. Although there may be a few boats tied up to the crumbling dock, you will walk on sagging planks, leap over gaps in the docking, and tightrope walk in some spots to reach the boats.

In Prickly Bay (the best hunting ground in Grenada) there is a short dock, and ample anchorage to dinghy around. There is the Boatyard Bar, a boatyard office with chandlery, the customs and immigration office, and a yacht grocery. You should get permission first to post notices, but the yard office and chandlery are pretty cooperative.

Prickly Bay is in a remote area of the island, and you must either take a taxi to and from (expensive), walk a few miles, or catch a van-type bus (cheap) that makes two regular daily trips to Prickly Bay.

It's best to search for crew positions on Grenada after the first of the year, when charter season gets into full swing and there's a lot of boat activity between the islands of the Grenadines. While it's a little more expensive to get around by land on Grenada, it is a must-see island and a good place to catch a boat heading down to Trinidad and Tobago, or Venezuela.

Venezuela is another popular cruising ground during the December-to-May cruising season, and many yachts will stop there before beginning a circumnavigation. Ask any yachtie in any of the Windward or Leeward islands about Venezuela, or head for the marinas and harbors there as you would any-where else.

The Mediterranean

Hundreds of private and charter boats from many European countries flock to the Mediterranean for the sailing season. Charter boats will finish the season in the Caribbean around the beginning of April and then gather for various "race weeks" on Barbados, Antigua, St. Thomas, Tortola (BVIs), and a hefty round of partying before heading back across the Atlantic to the Mediterranean during the months of April and May. Finding a good crewing position in the Mediterranean is not at all difficult if you start looking in April.

Yachts also cruise the south coast of Turkey, stopping in at Marmaris or Fethiye, and Cyprus. There are seemingly miles of dock to walk both in Marmaris and Fethiye, where boats tie up sometimes three deep. The docks are lined with one cafe or outdoor restaurant after another, and you can't help but trip over hundreds of yachties.

The islands of Rhodes, Corfu, and Crete all have customs offices, and all boats traveling around or through the Mediterranean, pleasure or charter, must check in with customs. In fact, you should find customs offices for all countries with major harbors listed in travelers' guidebooks. For the Mediterranean and the Aegean a great guide is *Baedeker's Greece*.

Mandraki Harbor, Rhodes, (where I concentrated my initial search) is home base for hundreds of private and charter boats. Not only can you walk the busy dock, you can also hang out at Popeyes', nestled way back in Old Town. In addition, there are sidewalk coffee and pastry shops, and a good-sized outdoor shopping and eating marketplace at the harbor where the yachties gather. You can post a notice at Camper & Nicholson's yacht services on Amerikis Street, a short walk up the hill into town, where many of the yachts in search of crew post notices.

Yacht owners and captains in Rhodes have said that Marseilles and Nice, along the south coast of France, are both excellent cruising spots with boats in abundance. I am told there is an agency called Peter Insull Yacht Marketing, based in Antibes, which acts as a contact point for professional crewmembers, such as experienced chefs, bartenders, and licensed captains, and puts them in touch with yacht owners looking for specific skills. So if you're an expert in your field and looking for a well-paid crewing position with a professional yachting concern, by all means try this agency.

Yachting season in the Mediterranean winds down around the end of September to early October, and boats get cleaned up, provisioned, and readied for the Atlantic crossing during the months of October and early November. This is an excellent time to secure a good crewing position for the passage to Gibraltar, with stops along the way first in either Italy or Sicily, or perhaps a port in Spain or the Canary Islands, then across the Atlantic.

Gibraltar

This is another great place to look for boats. Most boats crossing into or out of the Mediterranean stop in at Gibraltar for supplies, parts, provisions, and a rest.

You can walk the dock at Sheppard's Marina, or Marina Bay next to the runway, and The Anchorage on the far side of the runway. Don't forget to spend some time at the yachtie cafes located in the marinas. There are many marine supply stores at which to ask questions, post notices, and purchase foul weather gear before the Atlantic crossing.

Gibraltar may seem small, but it is packed with potential.

The Canary Islands

You need only be at Las Palmas, Gran Canaria, before the ARC race starts (on or around November 24th each year) to pick up a crewing position on one of the ARC race boats or any number of private yachts that have stopped for last-minute fuel, water, provisions, and crew changes before making the Atlantic crossing to the Caribbean. When you arrive, ask around for other areas of the Canary Islands where cruising yachts are likely to gather. Be sure to try Playa Las Americas in Tenerife as well.

The list of good places to look for a crewing position is long in and around the Caribbean and Mediterranean. For information on more than the areas listed in this book, contact the organization listed below for cruising guides of the areas in which you are interested. These cruising guides offer excellent information. For the information, as well as a good giggle, buy Chris Doyle's *Sailors Guide to the Windward Islands*, if you would like to crew in that area. Another good reference is the *Cruising Guide to the Virgin Islands*, (Simon and Nancy Scott, eds.) which, if you look for crewing assignments out of St. Thomas, will give you what you need to know about the Virgin Islands. Both books are available through Cruising Guide Publications, P.O. Box 13131 Sta. 9, Clearwater, Florida 34621 (813) 796-2469.

Plan to arrive at your desired cruising grounds early in the season. This way, you will have the opportunity to work on local charters and see the sights. And you'll make great contacts with skippers and yacht owners to ensure you a crew position on boats making longer passages.

A word of caution: The sailing community is a relatively small one and reputation plays a key role in your successful crewing lifestyle. Word of your skills and talents will travel fast, as will word of any misconduct—something to keep in mind.

As soon as you begin work on your first crew assignment, information will flow to you like a rushing river. Remember to ask questions of the experienced skippers about where and when boats sail. All boats follow the seasons and stay ahead of the cyclone seasons whenever possible.

Also among all good cruisers you will find some avid racers. The racing enthusiasts know when all of the major races occur around the world. Race boats usually do not carry their extra sails and equipment on board, but hire cruise yachts to go ahead of them to the race point. You may find a job on these cruisers and still travel with the racers at a more leisurely pace in this manner.

Well, that's all there is to it. Untangle your tangle, get your ducks in a row, pack your seabag, take a little money, and go where the boats float. You're on your way! Good sailing!!

TUCK THIS UNDER YOUR SAILOR'S HAT

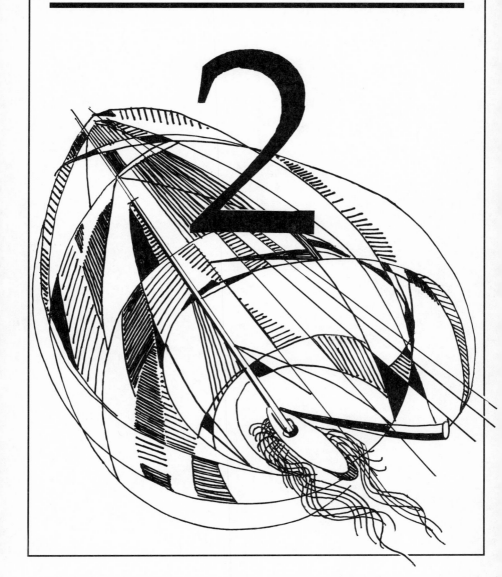

6

Do's and Don'ts

The first part of this guide was devoted to facts and figures. You might already be an old hand at sailing and traveling the world, so you only need to know the bare facts about entering and living the crewing lifestyle.

However, if you are currently an "establishment" non-sailor type looking to break into the sailing lifestyle on a permanent basis, there are some things which you should be aware of before you take the plunge.

You envision days of sheer perfection under the sun, with your bare feet on a deck. Swimming in tranquil crystal clear water. Hours of privacy to think and read and sleep. Tropical paradise. What you will find, along with all of the above delights, are some clouds inside the silver lining: clouds of frustration when equipment ceases to function, or the wind won't cooperate, or the work never seems to be done. Do not worry! You have probably experienced the same clouds on land and know that they'll blow over. You'll enjoy the sailing lifestyle—in some cases more than you expected!

The "be aware of" categories are placed in alphabetical order.

Boarding of Vessels

Now here is an experience you won't want to miss. When our vessel entered Italian and, later, Spanish waters, officials came alongside and boarded. The Italians boarded with much arm waving, shouting, and mixed instructions, and swarmed through the vessel, performing only a cursory search through random cupboards and under cushions. They spent most of their time poking through the laundry bag that contained fancy lacy underwear. They spoke no English and left the vessel rumpled and disordered. The Spanish officials boarded quietly, respectfully, and performed a very thorough search of all cupboards and holds, then apologized for the interruption and left the boat as they had found it.

These random boardings and searches as you approach or enter foreign ports are for drugs and firearms. Since you have nothing to hide, or shouldn't, allow the searchers to perform their duties and leave the vessel without undue fuss and disturbance. Cooperate with their questions by offering short, succinct answers. It is always best to allow the captain to answer all the questions regarding his/her vessel and cargo, the planned length of stay in the area, etc. Unless questions are directed to you, regarding you personally, refer the official to the captain.

The other type of boarding you will encounter is that of visitors. Often you will pull into a docking facility where boats are lined up alongside each other with fenders crushed so tightly between that your neighbor's deck is merely an extension of your own. Gangplanks are lowered and touch the dock with no gates, signs, or locks to keep out unwanted visitors. No matter how open and inviting, however, boats are still private property. Never board someone else's boat without permission from the captain or one of the crewmembers of that vessel. And never invite people you don't know to board your boat.

In most cases, your boat will be viewed with awe and envy by passers-by. In rare cases, you may be carefully watched by shadier characters for an opportunity to slip aboard and pick up a few things they see of value. Never leave your boat unattended for long periods of time without pulling up the gangplank and locking your hatches.

With so much activity taking place on a dock during a day, the chances are slim that you will be cleaned out. But even your neighbors can't keep track of who is and who is not allowed on your boat. Even though you're a crewmember of the vessel and not ultimately responsible for the equipment and possessions on board, it is your temporary home and you will naturally want to take some responsibility for its safety and yours.

Bugs and Crawlies

You will find them on land and, unfortunately, sometimes on the vessel on which you sail. If you are used to a bug-free environment at home, you will soon change your pristine attitudes when you sail. Cockroaches, spiders, lizards, ants, mosquitos, rats and mice, snakes, and a whole variety of flying or crawling things generously share their environment with visiting sailors and locals. You will often awake to find them camped in your room on land, or your cabin, or even snuggled into bed with you.

On my first morning on land in a rooming house on Bequia, I awoke staring down a giant cockroach. After a brief conversation with the critter, I ushered him out of my room. Later that night I met at least a hundred of his family members in the kitchen.

If you choose your boat carefully at the outset you should not be bothered by cockroaches on board. However, on land sometimes you'll have to co-exist with the beasties if not learn to be friends. Destructive though they may be to food and possessions, they rarely approach humans.

Mosquitos do make occasional visits to sailboats when the wind is not blowing hard. On sailboats you are bothered mostly when at the dock in marinas where strong winds are not present. You might need to fall asleep under a mosquito net or sheet to ward off squadrons of hungry mosquitos, unless you are anchored out in a stiff wind. Or, learn to live with a mosquito coil burning constantly.

Get used to your new friends and bunkies quickly because, more often than not, they will be more afraid of you than you of them. And, in most cases, they will not be harmful. You will be informed, usually by the locals, of what to watch out for and avoid.

Captains and Boats

Ah, here's the key to a successful outing. Choose your captain carefully. His/her boat can tell you a lot about his/her sailing knowledge and personality. Try to interview some current crewmembers of the vessel, or former crewmembers. Remember to take what's said with a grain of salt, as not all personalities will meld in harmony. But if three or four current or former crewmembers say the same things about the captain or vessel, you can bet those things will not change when you arrive on board.

Ask to tour the boat. If the boat is immaculate and organized, then it's possible the captain is a stickler for details and precision. You would work within rigid rules of sailing and organization.

Check the bilges. They should be clean and dry. On the second vessel I agreed to crew on, I had checked the bilges and was quite impressed with their pristine whiteness. I later learned that the job of keeping them that way was mine. I also later discovered that cleaning clean bilges was by far preferable to cleaning filthy bilges.

Look for rust or deterioration on the mast, turnbuckles, and chainplates. Check the condition of the sails. Keep an eye peeled for evidence of cockroaches or mice on board. If the boat is in disrepair, then the captain is likely to be inexperienced, which might endanger your life when the chips are down. Or he/she might be a superior sailor but a terrible "housekeeper," in which case you might learn a lot about sailing but live in filth while learning.

Sit down and have a chat with the captain you are considering—about sailing, about anything. The captain's personality will shine through. If he/she is alcoholic or dependent on drugs, the signs will be there and his/her continuous search for parties will be evident from the conversation. It is wise not to sail with a captain dependent upon drugs and drink unless you can navigate and handle the boat by yourself while the captain is sleeping it off.

Many of us who made the Atlantic crossing heard, upon arrival in Barbados, of a frantic crewie mid-Atlantic, attempting to hail any nearby boats for assistance as his captain had seriously short-circuited not too long after departure. Luckily for the vessel in distress, it connected eventually with another Caribbean-bound sailboat and followed it.

Two weeks to a month can seem like forever if you have chosen incorrectly. So take your time, look around, compare. There are plenty of crewing positions from which to choose.

Cardboard Boxes

Handy though they are to carry your provisions, *do not bring them on board*. Unload your provisions from the dinghy to someone waiting on deck; then promptly take your cardboard boxes and paper bags back to shore, and dispose of them properly. Why? Because little cockroaches take up residence in boxes and bags and set up a tidy family. When you store these cockroach homes on your boat, their inhabitants will venture out to explore their new surroundings and bring all of their

children. They find dark, moist parts of the boat preferable to their cardboard and paper homes, and you will have many new and quite unwelcome guests. Once you're infested with cockroaches, you're infested for good. No number of roach bombs or sprays will reach into the deep crevices of the bilges and floorboards and get them all. And as long as you have two roaches living aboard, you will soon have hundreds.

So throw out all cardboard boxes and paper bags, and make sure you remember first to wash stalks of bananas and bags of pineapples or citrus fruits in the sea, then to dip them into a bucket of fresh water containing a tablespoon of bleach.

Culture Shock

This is what happens when you leave home and all that is familiar, and toss yourself into foreign places, expose your ears to unfamiliar languages, start eating weird foods, and try adapting to a brand new lifestyle all at once. It is a temporary condition and easily cured.

After my first full month of traveling, I was scrubbing the deck of my second vessel, listening to several different languages being spoken on the neighboring boats and on the docks, when it suddenly occurred to me that I had not spoken a full sentence of my native English language in weeks. Culture Shock hit. I was desperate!

I had left the world of computers behind me, the jargon of *downloading* and *booting up* and *mainframes* and high-tech acronyms. I eagerly looked forward to discussing things like wind conditions, or the merits of one type of sailboat over another. I charged off the deck and went searching for a flag of an English-speaking country. I stopped at the flag of Greece when I heard English being spoken. I introduced myself to the friendly man who invited me for coffee and a chat. We talked computers for over two hours! The language never sounded better and I had gotten over my culture shock.

Drugs and Firearms

Neither is considered desirable or legal cargo, no matter what country you visit. Firearms can be carried only when permits are granted, and the captain must declare the firearms to customs and immigration upon checking in. Sometimes customs and immigration require that you leave the firearms with them while you cruise their territory.

The presence of firearms on board is rarely discussed openly, never advertised to strangers or neighboring yachties; and such things should always be kept in a safe place away from crew and guests.

Drugs are never allowed on board, and even a small amount found in your possession will land you in more trouble than the drugs are worth. The captain could be jailed as well, and his/her boat confiscated. So do not carry anything dangerous or illegal. And be extra careful, as you choose your boat, to watch for signs that other crewmembers may be carrying or using illegal drugs. Their trouble will be your trouble.

Etiquette

Sailing does not offer you a life of privacy. Everything you and other crewmembers do on board a sailboat, no matter what its size, can be seen or heard by other crewmembers and neighboring boats. You are a fish in a fishbowl.

While rafted up stern-to-bow with other boats three-deep in Mandraki Harbor, I decided that our boat, rafted on the outer end, was fairly private from passing tourists. The hot work day was over; I had taken my cool shower and then stretched out *au naturel* on my bunk to read and let the cool breeze blow across me from the overhead hatch. I was the only crewmember on board.

Before I had read the first sentence in the book, I heard a male voice say in a normal conversational tone, "Well, hello there." I sat up, peered upwards through the hatch, and returned a rather chagrined hello to the man sitting in his bosun's chair at the top of his mast two boats down from ours. He had been repairing a stuck halyard, not practicing voyeurism, and had a direct line of sight into my bunk.

Limit your noise. Wear your headphones to listen to your music unless the clients and the rest of the crew express their desire to share the sounds. If you rise early, keep your breakfast-making activities to a minimum. It's best to set everything up the night before, when everyone is awake, so that you can move quietly through the morning hours. If you are a screamer during sex, bite a pillow! You get the idea.

Sharing a cabin or bunk facilities in some cases means male crewmembers together, female crewmembers together, or male and female crewmembers together. It all depends on the size of the sailboat and available bunk facilities. Be kind to fellow bunkmates and keep your body aromas under control. Use soap and deodorants, but limit your after-shave or perfume scents in case your bunkmate has allergies. If a fellow bunkie snores, use your earplugs. It does no good to complain. Limit nudity if your bunkie is of the opposite sex and you are not romantically inclined toward that person. It's always good practice to discuss the sleeping arrangements and your peculiar habits as bunkies are being paired up.

Turn Japanese. In many parts of overcrowded Japan, total privacy cannot be had. Because everything is seen and heard on a sailboat as well, you will need to learn to close your ears, eyes and mouth on occasion. Paying guests are always right. Disagreements will occur, and at times tempers will run high. If you are not involved, stay out of it and go about your business. If you are involved in it, defer. Your discomfort will be short-lived, as paying guests stay only one to two weeks on board. Keep smiling.

Generally, fellow crewmembers respect the belongings of each other as well as those of other yachts. Locks on personal possessions are rarely used. However, it's never wise to leave your cash or expensive possessions lying around. Tuck them away and lock them up if you wish, but you shouldn't have any trouble with less tempting items. Crewmembers often exchange cassettes and share what they have brought. Keep track of where yours go, because when a crewmember leaves one boat for another, cassettes are the items most often lost in transit.

The captain is law. Crazy though some of them may be, the captain says what is and is not to be on board his/her boat. The first mate position also carries weight in the captain's absence. As crew, you must learn to follow orders. If, after you have given it your best try and turned the other cheek, you still cannot accept the sometimes unusual rules and regulations on a vessel, change vessels. Crew change boats regularly during a sailing season. You may wish to review the section entitled "Captains and Boats" for some important reminders.

Laundry must sometimes be done on board. Hanging your laundry on the lifelines is sometimes a necessity, but it carries an etiquette all its own. The easiest rule to remember is, try not to turn a marina slip into a laundry room; hang out discreet amounts of clothing at a time. Look around when you pull in to see if other boats have laundry hanging out. When you are anchored out, laundry is not usually a problem, and you can "let it all hang out" if necessary.

One female crewie on board had, without a doubt, the sexiest underthings of the entire crew, in lovely lavenders, racy reds, and passionate pinks. As ours was a charter boat, we made sure her laundry was hung prominently on the lifelines when we were docked in marinas where that was permitted. The sensuous colors attracted the dock-strolling sightseers, and we obligingly handed out our boat's brochure to the happy wanderers.

Many of the larger charter boats have a water heater on board that supplies a limited amount of hot water for dishes and showering. Allow the paying guests to shower first, whether they wish a hot or cool shower. In most cases, a cool or bracing cold shower is quite welcome because you will have perspired much during the warm days and also because you will need to rinse off the salt water from swimming. If charter guests are not involved, discuss the shower arrangements with fellow crewmembers. Sometimes on long passages showers are only allowed once a week. So don't count on always having a long, hot shower in the sailing lifestyle. However, many marinas provide excellent shower facilities to visiting yachts. Use those when possible.

Smoking is sometimes a problem on sailboats. You will encounter a mix of smokers and non-smokers. The captain sets the rules. Smoking is normally done only on deck on the downwind side so the smoke and ashes blow overboard. If you're a non-smoker, it will be important for you to find out the smoking rules on board. If you're a smoker, please be considerate. Many sailors enjoy the fresh air of the sailing lifestyle, and nothing can make tempers flare faster than a nose full of smoke.

The willingness of fellow yachties to lend a hand is the best part of this lifestyle. Yachties are a community unto themselves, and sharing and trading is part of the fun. If you see a boat pulling in, lend a hand with the lines, or help the crew settle their vessel comfortably alongside your boat in raft-up conditions.

Exchange your skills and knowledge with other yachties, lend a hand with repairs, but keep track of your tools. Tools are rarely stolen, but many are forgotten on someone's deck and end up overboard. You get the general idea: help your neighbors with what you can. Sometimes all they may need is information about the area, which you might be more familiar with. Or they might need a lift in your dinghy to their boat anchored out. Your smallest kindnesses are usually repaid twice over when you are in need of assistance.

Fish Poisoning

This is something to take careful note of. In many tropical areas, or areas where large concentrations of coral are found, fishing and eating what you catch is not a good idea. The local fish feed on the coral beds and ingest a type of poison that stays in their system. While it's not deadly to the fish, it can be to you. You'll most likely be told what fishes are good to eat locally, but the most sensible practice is not to fish and eat what you catch unless you do so out in the open ocean. Coral poisoning is most commonly found in tropical sailing grounds such as the French Polynesian and the Caribbean islands.

Nice to Know

As you become an experienced sailor you learn the value of experience. You know what can be put down a galley drain and what cannot. You know what type of toilet tissue the head tolerates, and how much of it, before repairs are needed. You also know that it is best *not* to throw anything but natural waste down the head.

You know how to conserve water on board by taking mini-showers. You know the importance of using biodegradable dish and laundry soap, shampoo, and other substances which go directly into the sea.

You know to separate biodegradable garbage from that which is not, and to empty your biodegradable garbage over the side far out to sea.

You know not to touch a boat's electronics unless you have received detailed instructions for each switch.

You know not to wear shoes on anyone's deck.

You know that flexibility and a willingness to turn the other cheek is appreciated. And, most of all, you know that a willingness to pitch in and work with the captain and other crewmembers is the most valuable asset you can possess as a crewmember.

And, if you did not know all that, you do now.

Nudity

Sailing offers a freedom of body and spirit that you do not often find on land. You will not last if you are a prude! Nudity on deck while sailing is quite common for both men and women. Showering nude on deck is sometimes a necessity— and always a welcome treat in hot climates!

When clients are aboard a charter vessel on which you are crew, it's best to let them set the pace regarding nudity. If they show no interest in removing their clothing, then please keep yours on. Everyone will be more comfortable that way, and, after all, they are paying for the vacation and your expertise as crew.

A minimum amount of body covering is recommended on deck while you're anchored out, but be more modest in a slip at a marina. When you go ashore or set foot on a dock, the minimum clothing allowable is a shirt and shorts for both men and women, and some type of shoes. In some countries, both men and women are required to wear long-sleeved shirts and slacks with the minimum of skin showing. Inquire about local customs.

Please do not wear your bikini, short shorts, or skimpy clothing on land in any country. You will be informed either by the captain of the vessel, by reading the cruising guide for that area, or by the customs and immigration officials as you check in, what the appropriate attire is for that country.

Provisioning

Ice does not last long on a sailboat. If you crew on a boat that has continuous refrigeration, then provisioning poses fewer problems. You can keep eggs, bacon, butter, milk, cheese— anything needing refrigeration—fresh for as long as the refrigeration works on the sailboat. Boats using block ice require a bit more planning and food care.

First, discuss with the captain where you will be sailing for at least three days, and when you will be able to reprovision. The captain will know in which anchorages there will be restaurants. The captain usually discusses the restaurant situation with the charter clients and crew to determine how many meals they wish to eat on board and how many in restaurants for the week.

Buy only those "keep cool" provisions you'll use for breakfasts and lunches (usually eaten on board) from provisioning stores in the anchorages.

Always keep a supply of rice, pastas, spaghetti, canned spaghetti sauce, fresh garlic, onions, oregano, curry, canned tomatoes, canned tuna, grated Parmesan cheese, canned fruit, olive oil, vinegar, instant coffee, mustard and mayonnaise, bottled water, and canned ham or luncheon meat in dry storage. From these simple supplies you'll always be able to scare up an edible meal in a pinch when meal plans take an unexpected turn or the refrigeration goes on the blink. (See Chapter 7 for meal suggestions.)

Fresh bread should be purchased daily when your boat is near a village. In warm climates, bread molds quickly. When you won't be near a fresh bread supply for two or three days, keep your loaves, usually two, in a plastic bag, but leave the bag open and store the bread inside a cupboard. Lay in a small supply of packaged toast and crackers just in case the bread goes bad.

The groceries you buy will most likely be packed in a plastic carrying bag. Save the bags. They're good for storing biodegradable garbage, which gets dumped into the sea on long sails offshore. The bags themselves stay on board until you reach a land disposal site. The bags are also good for preserving leftovers.

To provision for cool storage, plan on a lot of cheese, butter, yogurt, at least a dozen eggs, fresh fruit, and as many different vegetables as you can find. Meat and poultry should be purchased after discussion regarding preferences of fellow crewmembers and guests. Meat and poultry does not keep more than a few days if purchased fresh, and a week at best when kept frozen, because freezing temperatures on boats are not consistent. Chocolate bars are always a nice treat once in a while, but must be kept cold.

Questions

Never stop asking them of everyone you meet—locals, other yachties—about their home countries, the people, their likes and dislikes, where they have traveled. You will learn more than you expected you ever would. Everywhere you travel, the locals are usually always eager to learn English and to share information about their country or their customs.

When you pull into a remote anchorage and get served by someone who speaks a little English, take the time to get to know them. One Turkish waiter I met in Kapi, a little anchorage along the south coast of Turkey, was a botanical engineer during the winter when the yachting season was over, and another waiter was a marketing manager.

Ask skippers and crew on other yachts how long they have sailed and where. Ask them about the seasons to sail and the places to avoid. Watch how they handle their boats in all situations, and learn as much as you can about sailing, cooking, and general maintenance while crewing. Good crew are highly valued.

Sailing at Night

Night watches are probably the most relaxing *and* energizing experience you will ever have. On night watches, you will still be able to see what is in front of and behind you from reflected starlight or moonlight. The light comes from somewhere, anyhow. You will learn how to determine which way a passing ship is going by the pattern of lights. And how to avoid getting turned into toothpicks by those passing ships by maneuvering to port or starboard, then returning to course.

You'll have radar, in some cases, to warn you of approaching land masses or moving ships. Radar requires that you run belowdecks periodically to study the radar screen—it doesn't tap you on the shoulder or call out your name. And you'll have a quiet time to study the stars, listen to some music on your headphones (removing them occasionally to listen to the boat sounds), and to exercise. If the seas are calm and the winds are light, you might have an autopilot to steer for you, if it's working and the captain is agreeable to its use.

In any case, you do keep moving at night on long passages, so be prepared for a beautiful and exciting experience. Make sure you get at least one or two watches where you can see the sunrise!

Sailing Opportunities

You know by now that charter work offers the biggest category of crewing positions. These positions, as cook, hostess, and deckhand often involve payment for your labor as well as providing your bunk and all meals consumed on board. The work is not only physically but mentally demanding. Charter customers who are normally mild-tempered and agreeable on land might turn into demanding royalty for one or two weeks when on a sailboat. They want their lemons cut "just so," make outrageous demands, and treat you less than courteously.

Other charter customers can be a sheer delight to be around as they discover the pleasures of sailing and relaxing in incomparable scenery and mingling with people who can teach them about a different way to live and enjoy life. They are eager to learn to sail and tell you about their lifestyle at home. Charter work is only one of the opportunities open to you to see the world from the deck of a boat.

Private yachts are another way to crew your way around. Many owners of large luxury yachts use them only occasionally. In these cases, a captain and crew are hired to keep the boat moving about the world to wait for the owner's arrival at various locations. These yachts may occasionally entertain friends of the captain, and you may be called upon to act as a steward or cook. In other cases, the owner is the captain, and he/she is on board continuously.

As previously mentioned, crewing positions are either paid or labor-exchange positions. Your bunk is provided, as are your meals on board, and captains are often generous when it comes to buying dinners for their crew on land. Even though you may not earn money, depending upon the crewing positions and boat, you will not spend much either, and you still get to see many parts of the world from the deck of a boat.

When looking for crewing assignments, don't forget the sail race circuit. Any major sail-oriented magazine will list the major races of the world and their schedules. Go to the area where the race is to begin, and ask around for crewing positions. You may get on a racing yacht or a chase yacht that carries the equipment. You may or may not get paid, depending upon the boat or your position on it.

Another way to travel is by private yacht, where the owner is captain and asks that you share expenses. In many cases like this, the captain may be looking for a long-term "significant other" with which to share his/her sailing life as well as expenses.

Also, the private yacht may be a good way for you to get to a desired location for less than it would cost if you traveled alone by other means. If you don't mind becoming a financial contributor, you can perhaps meet your future lifemate and see the world together. Keep in mind that this is also a good way for you to be taken advantage of, both physically and financially. Do a lot of research and checking up on the captain and the vessel before entering deals such as this.

This book concentrates on the general crewing lifestyle and duties primarily for sailboats. There are, however, many large luxury powerboats cruising the world. They employ experienced seamen/women, and crewmembers wear uniforms and get paid healthy salaries. The lifestyle is less free, and the work is more regimented and equitably distributed, but if you are so inclined you might want to explore the possibilities of crewing on a luxury powerboat. These powerboats can be found in many of the same marinas and anchorages as the cruising sailing yachts.

There are always positions available in the world of sailing for experienced licensed captains, navigators, mechanical and electrical repair-persons, refrigeration specialists, engine specialists, sailmakers, and professional chefs. Once you get involved in the sailing lifestyle and start looking around, if you're a qualified professional, you'll soon find these jobs. Again, this book is designed as a starter guide for general crewing.

Shoes

Rarely will you wear shoes, even deck shoes, when on deck unless you are working with tools or the anchor. Shoes worn on land pick up little pebbles, shards of glass, burs and spurs, and when those are tracked across a deck the results can be discouraging. Always remove your shoes before walking on anyone's deck, just as a habit. Your hosts will be grateful. (Remember to wear your rubber flip-flops in unfamiliar public showers, to avoid contracting foot diseases.)

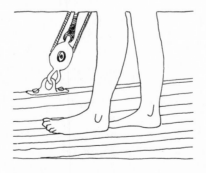

Swimming

As you sail from one location to the next you will either read about or learn from fellow travelers what to watch out for when you swim. While much of the world's water will be crystal clear, blue, green, or turquoise, and always inviting, there might be some danger.

Never swim wearing anything sparkling, like jewelry. This can attract barracuda and shark.

Wear a protective foot covering and a diving mask if you plan to swim to shore and walk in the sand. Many shorelines are lined with spiny sea urchins, stinging coral, stone fish, or an occasional stingray. The cruising guides or information booklets about each area to which you sail will mention the swimming hazards particular to that area. Please read and take note before you jump in.

Remember not to swim in harbors or small anchorages where a lot of boats are gathered and where there is no water exchange from the open ocean. Pollution is a sad fact of life, and swimming in a polluted anchorage or harbor could cause serious illness or even death.

One special note here regards sandy beaches. In the Greek Islands the beaches are gravel, coarse sand, or sometimes lava ash. It is quite common after lying on these beaches to contract a virus of the skin that shows up as little white polka dots against your tan. To protect yourself against these bacteria, be sure to keep a beach towel or your pareu between you and the sand or gravel beaches.

Values and Beliefs

You might be presented with a world upside-down from that which you experienced on land. The sailing lifestyle is one without written rules and regulations governing personal conduct. Your values and beliefs will be tested daily.

Conduct yourself from the very first day of your new lifestyle in a way consistent with how you would wish to be regarded and accepted from that day forward. News travels fast throughout the sailing community. Reputations, both good and bad, are noted, and gossip is a way of life. Drinking is heavy and frequent. Drugs are available. You can buy into the frenzy and indulge until you drop. Or you can pace yourself and enjoy life longer. Mother will not be there to tell you what to do.

Weather Conditions

Land areas in the Aegean Sea, between Athens and Turkey, along the south coast of Turkey and the Mediterranean countries, are hot during the months of June, July, and August. Temperatures can reach as high as 114° F. This is a baking heat, and you will feel as if you have popped into an oven to roast.

The Caribbean islands during the July, August, and September off-peak months are steamy hot. You will be in a constant sauna. Expect to perspire a lot. Whether the heat is dry or steamy, you will most likely feel sluggish and tired during the mid-afternoon hours. (Temperatures are slightly cooler and the winds are stronger in the months of January, February and March.)

Plan ahead for the excessive heat during the mid-afternoon hours by performing your heavier work activities in the early morning and later afternoon or evening hours. Rest in a shady area during the mid-afternoon hours. Wear a hat even though it might make you a degree warmer; the sun sucks the moisture from your body rather quickly. Drink three quarts or more of water or non-alcoholic liquids per day. Use sunscreen lotions and even sun blocks. Take vitamins. Dress in light clothing that lets the air circulate.

Although on land you might be hot, should you make an Atlantic crossing when migrating with the yachts from season to season, you'll need some warm clothing. Temperatures do drop around October and November during the crossing, occasional storms pop out of nowhere—and that's when your foul weather gear comes in handy. Don't skimp, buy a good-quality jacket, bib-type overalls, and boots. Look for a warm lining, heat-sealed seams, and snaps or Velcro closers around ankles, wrists, and neck. (I found the Douglas Gill brand to be effective and reasonably priced.) You'll also need a waterproof hat or hood, and a pair of thermal socks. This gear is great on deck and you can peel down to normal clothing if belowdecks is warmer and drier.

If you're not planning to make long passages, but stay instead in the warm climates around one area, you may not need to buy or carry foul weather gear at all. It's better first to start your sailing lifestyle, see where you want to concentrate your sailing time, and then buy warmer clothing or foul weather gear accordingly.

Work

This can prove a touchy area for some who think the sailing lifestyle is one of constant partying and leisure. When you work as crew, whether entertaining guests on a charter boat during the height of season or preparing for the Atlantic crossing, or on a private cruising yacht, or even on a circumnavigation, there will always be work to be done on board. Because of salt water, constant movement, and chafing of parts, boats require continuous care and maintenance.

The work can be hard and dirty, like scrubbing decks, bilges, and heads (toilets). Or it can be strenuous, like hauling around heavy sails and equipment, or sanding and varnishing wood. Or it can be tedious, like constantly polishing brass and scrubbing headliners and wiping off surfaces. No matter, boats are always a lot of work. And work is not always "fairly" distributed among crewmembers.

It seems the rule rather than the exception, that on every boat one crewmember inevitably takes on the role as the captain's playmate, while the other crewmembers keep the boat shipshape. Since the crewing lifestyle offers constant opportunity for change, on one boat you may be left to the scrubbing and the lion's share of the work, while on another you may "sign on" as the captain's playmate. The capacity in which you travel on a sailboat is entirely left to your personal values and morals.

Just remember, if you travel as a worker, you still enjoy all the pleasures of the sailing lifestyle: a refreshing wash-down after the work is finished, personal pride in a job well done, a cool drink, a tasty dinner, and a relaxing sunset. And workers have ample time to learn about the countries, and the people, and to sightsee along with the playmates. Workers do meet and mingle constantly with fellow yachties and have ample time and opportunity to "play" as well. Besides, no one ever said life was fair.

7

Who Says You Can't Cook?

You don't have to be a gourmet chef in order to satisfy the hungry guests and crew on board a boat. You should know how to boil water and be able to tell when something should be cooked or served raw. If you have some basic cooking and serving skills you'll do fine on a sailboat.

Very few charter guests or fellow crewmembers look for huge hearty breakfasts of greasy bacon or fried potatoes or pancakes, which might weigh them down and make them sluggish in the water. Because sailing is relaxing and lacking in strenuous exercise, breakfasts and lunches are usually kept light and varied.

The French set the pace for some very satisfying breakfasts and lunches on board that please all nationalities. They eat simply, but well. A basic breakfast consists of fresh sliced bread, one or two fried or soft boiled eggs, yogurt, fresh fruit, boxed toast or biscuits, butter and jam, coffee and/or tea.

After a morning of swimming, snorkeling, shell collecting, or walking around exploring the land, a medium-weight lunch on board is a welcome meal. If you haven't discussed any special meal requirements of your guests or crew, or have had no specific requests made, you can usually please a crowd by laying out the following:

- ○ Cheeses, a good variety of hard and soft

- ○ Fresh bread

- ○ Butter

- ○ Luncheon meats or pâtés

- ○ Tuna, either plain from the can or mixed with mayonnaise o Tossed salad, carrot salad, pasta salad, or marinated raw veggies

o Hard-boiled eggs, plain and deviled with mayo and spices

o Fresh fruit (whatever is available at the local market)

o Left-over "whatever" from the night before if you cooked dinner and yummy morsels remain

o Bottled water

o Red or white wine

o Beer

o Soft drinks

While your guests and crew are occupied with early morning activities, you can prepare the various salads and marinated veggies before you jump in for your own morning swim and snorkel session.

Later in the evening your guests and fellow crew will most likely be ready for a heartier meal. Fresh air, salt water, sunshine, exercise, and relaxation can do wonders for an evening appetite! If a restaurant is close at hand, you and the rest might pack off to it for an evening of eating, drinking, and being merry. On the rare occasions you find yourself without a restaurant, there's no need to panic. Again, a gourmet meal is less important than a filling, tasty one, and people learn to make do in a pinch.

You'll always be carefully instructed regarding special dietary considerations of your guests and crew, and you should prepare your meals accordingly. It's not unusual to prepare two separate meals to place on the same table to adjust to the special needs of the diners. All it really boils down to is more cleanup, not necessarily more cooking expertise.

A special note may be in order here about varying degrees of ability to cook. On smaller, independent charter boats, your cooking skills need not be dynamic. However, on some larger, corporation-owned charter boats a quality chef with the ability to plan, prepare, and present gourmet meals is of the utmost importance. Again, if you plan on signing on as cook, be sure to ask the captain what his requirements are regarding what his guests expect.

This short chapter contains some easy, hearty meal suggestions that seem to appeal to all tastes. Remember, before you add strong spices or garlic to a recipe, be sure everyone to whom you serve it likes that particular flavor.

A few favorites also serve well the next day as a cold salad when the weather is hot and a cold meal is welcome. The ingredients are simple and can usually be found in your storage cupboards. You can use whatever is on hand and your own imagination to create meals. Amounts of each ingredient depend on the size of the crowd you're feeding and their taste buds.

Think pasta salad. This filling dish can be served with a variety of cheeses, fresh fruit (grapes, sliced apples, peeled orange slices), crackers, wine, beer, soft drinks, coffee or tea. Leftovers can be served for lunch the next day. Store leftovers in refrigeration and the next day add a touch of olive oil and a touch of vinegar to restore moisture—and a dash of fresh oregano.

Spiced rice is another hearty favorite. This one is fun when the captain surprises you with a change of dinner plans. Think fast! In 25 minutes (cooking time) you have a hot dinner—a simple one-pot concoction of rice, veggies, canned tuna or browned meats, and spices. Mix them all together in a large pot and bring to a boil. Cover and let simmer. It makes a lot, but comes out a little soupy, so serve in a bowl (or use one-half cup less water to cook).

Serve with a green salad, or sliced fresh tomatoes and cucumbers splashed with a dash of olive oil, sliced fresh bread, or even garlic toast. Store leftovers in refrigeration and the next day—you guessed it—a little olive oil and a little vinegar mixed in makes a great cold salad for lunch!

Spaghetti is a never-fail crowd pleaser. If you don't have a jar of prepared spaghetti sauce handy on board, use canned tomato sauce and drop in some chopped onions, mushrooms, browned meat, garlic, oregano, and basil, and simmer it for a bit. Follow the boiling instructions on the spaghetti package and serve the lot with garlic bread, a green salad, or a green vegetable. Don't forget the grated Romano or Parmesan cheese, and bottles of red and white wine.

The above-mentioned are the simplest and quickest dishes to present when plans change or you aren't near a handy restaurant. Other meals that you do plan to prepare on board can be a little more elegant, but may not necessarily require more work.

Roasted chicken with potatoes and veggies is a one-baking-pan affair and a general favorite. Set a whole chicken into a deep baking pan. Stuff it loosely with a mixture of cooked rice, spices, raisins, or nuts, and surround it with quartered potatoes, onions and carrots. Baste everything liberally with butter or olive oil, sprinkle oregano and parsley over it all, and pop it into the oven to bake for about an hour and a half at 350°. Test the chicken by pulling gently at a leg. It should separate easily from the body when it's perfectly cooked. Remember to baste the lot at least every 20 minutes, and turn the potatoes and other veggies to keep them moistened with the cooking oils. Serve with a green salad, or sliced tomatoes and cucumbers sprinkled with olive oil. Fresh sliced bread. Wine.

This same procedure can also be used for roasting meats like beef or pork roasts. Or you can prepare the veggies separately and serve mashed potatoes. Make gravy from the roast drippings by adding a cup of water, a touch of flour or (preferably) cornstarch, a dash of teriyaki or soy sauce, a bouillon cube, and some spices.

And what dinner table on a sailboat would be complete without fish dishes? There are so many ways to prepare fish—the trick is not to overcook it. Fish takes literally minutes when browned in a skillet, and no more than a half hour when baked in an oven. Sauce it, stuff it, bread it, spice it!

Almost everyone has a favorite recipe, so don't be shy about asking for some from fellow crewies and guests. Serve fish with rice or a baked potato, tossed green salad, and a green veggie like green beans or broccoli. Easy to cook. Easy to serve. Easy to clean up the dishes.

So there you have a pasta dish or two, rice dish, meat, poultry, and fish. If you are to take on the duties of full-time cook for a long passage, you might want to pick up a copy of Michael Greenwald's *The Cruising Chef Cookbook*. Write to Michael Greenwald, 421 Gerona Avenue, Coral Gables, FL 33146. The book is thick and heavy, but paperback, and well worth carrying along. In Greenwald's book, not only do you get recipes designed for the sailing life, but information on proper cleaning and storage of food items, and on pressure cooking, which is invaluable on a boat with limited water reserves. If that book is no longer available, you can find others in the book section of your local chandlery or bookstore.

The suggestions in this chapter work well if you are the cook on an island-hopping cruise. Should you find yourself signed on for longer open-ocean passages, you'll need to think ahead and adjust your meals according to the weather and on-board conditions.

For instance, much as I would have preferred to turn out a turkey with all the fixings to celebrate not only Thanksgiving, but our first day out across the Atlantic, vegetable soup was all I could prepare. The seas were rough and the crew was queasy after seven calm days in Madeira. I barely got the ingredients into a pot on a gimble-mounted stove before the heat and rough bucking belowdecks sent me scampering topsides into cold fresh air. As it turned out, I was in better shape than the rest of the crew, who could not remotely entertain the idea of eating. The turkey dinner was not missed.

Trial and error over a two-week period of time will produce a workable menu for calm to rough weather. Don't be afraid to try different dishes.

Happy cooking and *bon appétit*!

8

Yo Ho Ho–A Pirate's Life

If you're a seasoned sailor, most of the information in this chapter will be familiar. But for you novice crewmembers, it outlines some very important skills, and useful knowledge that will make your crewing experience more enjoyable.

Without sugar coating—there's a heavy dose of good old-fashioned chauvinism that goes along with sailing. If you're a man, you will most likely be "the sailor" handling the helm, hoisting and trimming the sails, hauling the heavy stuff. If you're a woman, no matter how strong or experienced a sailor you are, or how much deckhand work you have done, you will most likely end up in charge of the galley, cleaning belowdecks, and serving coffee when you cruise on someone else's boat. So be prepared. Remember, there are exceptions to every rule. On my first crewing assignment I was the cook/hostess. On my second crewing assignment I was the first mate on a 76-foot sloop. Whether cook or deckhand, however, all of the following applies to both men and women.

If you don't possess basic sailing skills, nor learned any before taking off for a life of cruising, there are still many captains who will hire you or take you on as crew because they prefer to train a novice to do things their way. So don't think you absolutely must know the basics, as there are some boats you can actually learn on. And, please, don't lie about your level of experience, or you may find yourself in over your head—literally.

The Head

First and foremost, don't throw toilet paper or any other substance other than natural waste down the marine toilet, unless okayed by the captain. It will, guaranteed, break down or clog up. Marine toilets are touchy and sometimes will not even digest natural waste material. Always flush with plenty of water. Just because the bowl is clear, the connecting hoses may not be, and that's where the trouble begins.

There are many different types of marine toilets available from worldwide manufacturers. Be sure you read all instructions and ask questions of the skipper on special operating instructions for each different toilet you encounter. On five different makes of boats on which I sailed, I encountered five different makes of marine toilets. None of them required an engineering degree to figure out.

Water Conservation

Fresh water on sailboats of any size is precious. Use it sparingly. You might have a few hundred gallons of water on board and the water pump could break! Unless the captain tells you that water is no problem, here are some important guidelines regarding fresh water usage and conservation on sailboats.

DISHES First remove heavy grease, butter, and food scraps from skillets, pots, dishes, and silverware with a paper towel. Then dip a large bucket into the sea and scrub everything with seawater and biodegradable soap, and rinse with seawater, either in the galley sink or right up on the deck. (That saves trips belowdecks with a heavy sloshing bucket. This method, of course, is not advisable in high seas or strong winds). You'll find that many boats, especially larger ones, are equipped with a seawater foot pump and spigot right at the galley sink, which makes life much easier for the dishwasher. A note of caution is in order here regarding using seawater— use it only where there is a continuous exchange of fresh seawater, not in crowded, polluted marinas!

Finally, fill the galley sink part way with fresh water and perform a final rinse of the items with fresh water. Use paper plates when possible to save water on longer voyages.

Before you drain the rinse water, make sure you've used it to wipe down any soiled counter tops, the stove, or salon table. Also, if the water is still clean, you can rinse out a few items of laundry.

LAUNDRY   Again, wash items first with biodegradable detergent in a bucket of seawater to scrub out the heavy dirt. Perform the final rinse with fresh water, and look around for ways to use the rinse water before draining it. It's good for wiping down fiberglass surfaces or removing salt residue from the deck and rigging.

SHOWERS   Here is the biggest water waster of all if you're not familiar with seamen's showers. To use the least amount of water possible and yet come out squeaky clean, use a hand-held shower head if one is available. On larger boats you may find a fixed shower head, but the method is still the same: First, wet your hair while standing up (if possible) so that the water runs down your body. Then shut the water off. Use a biodegradable shampoo sparingly and lather your hair. While you still have shampoo on your hands, you can use it as soap, and/or you can rub your body down with a bar of soap and a sponge. After you've thoroughly scrubbed from head to toe, turn the shower on and direct the water from your head first, and rinse down to your toes. Then shut the water off again. That's it. You're clean, and you have used only a minimum amount of water. On long passages, the skipper should always advise you how much water is to be used per day by each crewperson and for what purposes. If he/she doesn't, be sure to ask.

Here's a handy hint that worked for the crew on our Atlantic crossing when something unexpected happened to our water supply. We had bought bottled water to drink while on land in Madeira, then filled the empties with tap water from the marina supply. We stored the extra bottled water in our bunks (perhaps as much as 20 gallons total between all crewies) for just-in-case. A day and a half away from Barbados, with land in sight, our captain shut off the water supply because of a leaky pump. Out came our emergency bottled water for showers and teeth. When it comes to fresh water on board, expect the unexpected and be prepared!

TEETH   Brushing is important, and you probably won't want to do that with seawater. Brush your teeth as you would take a shower. Turn the water on to wet the brush, then turn it off. Fill half a small glass with fresh water, and after you are through scrubbing your teeth, use the glass of water to rinse out your mouth and the sink.

LITTLE CLEANUPS   Sailing can be a messy business. Handling lines, grinding winches, cooking, wiping down surfaces, and anything else you do during the day that involves your hands will no doubt produce some dirt. Fill a small bucket with seawater and keep it in the galley sink. With biodegradable soap, scrub the grime off in the bucket of seawater. If you have a double sink, fill a second small bucket or pot with fresh water and dip your hands to rinse off. This water can be used all day. Remember—before you drain the rinse water, make sure you can't make good use of it for something else.

Garbage

Some sailors don't care what happens to their environment and will indiscriminately trash the oceans and beaches. Out in the middle of the Atlantic, with no land in sight, I watched plastic beverage containers and plastic bags float by.

Separate all biodegradable substances from non-biodegradable; only those that biodegrade will go overboard. The rest is bagged and stored until you reach a refuse container on land. Setting up two disposal bins on board takes no extra effort or time. Clearly label each one. On one French vessel I taped a sign on the top of one container, *Pour les Poissons* (translated: For the Fish). It was effective, and everyone participated in garbage separation as a result.

It *is* okay to dump into the ocean all food scraps, paper (not waxed or plastic coated) plates, other paper products, uncapped glass bottles, wadded-up aluminum foil, paper napkins, paper bags, cardboard torn into small pieces, open aluminum and other metal cans. You get the idea.

It *is not* okay to dump plastic bottles, plastic bags, plastic cups or tableware, styrofoam (a *big big* no-no), or anything else that will not dissolve in water over a short period of time. The fish the world depends upon for food, and the sea mammals that will entertain and educate you, will appreciate your extra efforts to keep their home safe.

Shipshape

Sailboats, no matter what size, get cluttered quickly with clothing, cups, newspapers, empty soft-drink cans, whatever. Be aware and tidy up. To combat condensation and food particles that may draw crawly critters, wiping down surfaces is always a good idea. So be neat and lend a hand to keep things shipshape, whether you are cook, hostess, or captain.

Host/Hostess

Every boat needs at least one. If your job is host/hostess as part of the crew, graciousness is the best skill. Keep a casual eye on the guests and the captain. Watch for special meal requirements, remember what each guest prefers to drink, and offer refreshments when you think mouths are becoming parched.

On the first French vessel I sailed, I learned the phrases in French for "Would you like something to eat (or drink)," which greatly pleased the guests and made their stay (and mine) that much more enjoyable. By the end of the two-week cruise I had learned enough French phrases not only to handle the job as cook/hostess, but for most of the parts of the boat! Don't be afraid to try a new language. It's all part of your new lifestyle.

Many people don't snack between meals, but perhaps a half-hour to an hour before lunch or dinner you might want to put out an hors d'oeuvre tray of crackers and cheese, a variety of nuts in the shell, or a bowl of fresh fruit. The smell of cooking stirs the hunger, and a handy munchie or two will keep the customers happy until the meal is on the table.

Aside from food and beverage duties, be aware that heads may need to be resupplied with toilet paper, boxes of tissue, or soap.

Watch for towels that begin to smell a bit musty due to incomplete drying between uses, bed sheets that need changing during a longer cruise, ashtrays that need emptying, surfaces that need wiping to remove spilled makeup, scattered cigarette ashes, or other substances.

Check the area around guest toilets frequently and wipe down with a disinfectant. In a plunging sea or tilted vessel, guests may not always find it easy to get their aim straight. Run a paper towel dampened with a window cleaner over mirrored surfaces and a dampened sponge over the cabin sole when possible as well.

Shopping For Food

You can always find a bargain! If your job is to shop for the provisions, the best thing is to ask the captain where he/she has found the best stock for the lowest prices. Experienced captains who have operated charter vessels in a particular area for more than one season usually know. If not, however, take a day and stroll through the various marketplaces available at each major town or village in which you stop. (If the boat you are currently crewing on doesn't need to provision at this stop, perhaps a future boat on which you work will).

In Rhodes I had the dubious pleasure of shopping for

provisions at the end of what must have been a long and tiring tourist season for the locals. It was during this harrowing outing that I learned that "please," "excuse me," and "I'm sorry" do not seem to be used, especially in supermarkets. Instead, shoppers play a game. You get your blue shopping basket, sling it over your arm, and see how many tourists, locals, and women named Maria you can knock out of the way before you yourself get nailed by a small, wily, 90-year-old with vast experience.

In Madeira, provisioning is a different story. I spent the better part of a day wandering happily through a giant two-story open market that displayed fresh fruits from the exotic to common, vegetables, fresh chicken and meats, cut flowers, baskets—everything your boat could need and then some.

When you go comparison shopping, take a small notebook and jot down the name of the store, the location, and the prices of the most commonly used items on boats. Also carry a small dictionary of English-Spanish, English-French, or English-Whatever-Language-They-Speak so you will be able to read product labels when there are no pictures on the box to guide you.

When not at sea, you will most always purchase fresh bread first thing in the morning for that day's meals. If you're crewing in a foreign country, this procedure is fairly standard. If you're crewing where bread comes in neat slices and wrappers, you may want to purchase extra loaves and store them in a freezer. Remember that food items collect mold very fast on a sailboat, so buy only what you will use between provisioning stops.

If your job is provisioning, be prepared to spend a full day on this task, especially when provisioning before an ocean crossing or other long passage. Once you buy the food, you'll also need to clean it, sort it, perhaps catalog it, and stow it. Don't hesitate to use a taxi to haul your purchases back to the boat if you have no other means of transporting the heavy groceries. Taxi fares are not that expensive (but always negotiate the price before you climb in) and the drivers are usually most helpful in handing you the bagged goods as you stand on deck.

Mechanical Skills

You don't have to know how to repair engines—although that is a valuable skill. Simple mechanical skills which are a must include knowing where the valves are for the water tanks and how to use them properly. Each boat is different, so put this on your list of things to ask about when you are hired on.

If there's an auxiliary generator for charging the boat's batteries or running electrical systems when the engine is off, you should know how to start and stop it.

Learn the proper procedure for regulating the refrigeration systems, checking the water pressure, and handling the navigation instruments and lights. Usually all toggle switches are clearly marked for purpose and on/off positions.

If you're in port for any length of time and are using shore (electrical) power, make sure you know how to switch from battery to shore power properly. The proper handling and care of electronics on a boat is critical to the functioning of the boat, and EACH BOAT IS DIFFERENT. Please do not assume because you did something one way on one boat, you will do it the same on the next vessel. Ask the skipper.

Learning the basic mechanics of a boat's systems takes only minutes and can save major problems and expensive repairs.

It's also a good idea to "tune in" to the various sounds a sailboat produces. When the engine is running or the generator is charging and functioning properly, take note. The minute the pitch changes, or a strange grinding begins, or any other sound that might be signaling trouble starts, tell your captain or the first mate. If no one is around, that's when your knowledge of how to properly shut down the engine or the generator comes in handy.

It most often happens that the minute the captain and crew leave the vessel, the water tanks run dry. A dry tank is signaled by the electric fresh water pump running nonstop and the water either coughing out of the faucets or ceasing to run altogether. A water pump should not be allowed to run dry. During such an emergency you need to know the location of the valves that switch from one tank to another. Be sure to tell the captain upon his/her return that you changed water tanks, so that they can keep track when a refill is necessary.

Keep in mind that everyone makes mistakes. In spite of my having asked a multitude of careful questions and having received expert instruction on the electrical panel, I almost sank one boat somewhere out in the Peloponnese. There were two toggle switches, one above the other, which controlled two separate bilge pumps. One bilge pump (in a shower) was malfunctioning and had to be manually switched on and off periodically. The other pump (in the engine compartment) was functioning properly on automatic. It was my responsibility as first mate to watch the shower bilge and drain as necessary. So, I carefully checked the shower bilge, noted that it was full, flipped the wrong bilge switch—and an hour later scrambled with the rest of the crew to drain the engine compartment before the water level doused the engine! Check and double check your procedures—one little mistake could cost you the boat or your life. If in doubt, don't touch!

The Engine

Very important. Although you have sails to carry you across the ocean blue, the engine on a sailboat plays a very important role. It gets you into and out of anchorages safely in strong winds. It gets you across the ocean when the wind fails to blow. It rescues you from tight situations when all the sails want to do is fill with wind and blow you sideways into some solid object. And it charges your batteries for electrical power.

So learn how to use the blowers, glow plugs, starters, stoppers, keys, buttons, knobs, and whistles on each boat you sail, including the motorized dinghies. Engine operation is not difficult. Ask your captain and all will be well. It's also good to work a little with the gears and throttle if your captain feels your hand on the helm during the passage will be required. If you can drive a car with success, you can handle the engine work on a boat with a touch of practice.

There, the basics aren't so bad, are they? You'll learn more as you sail.

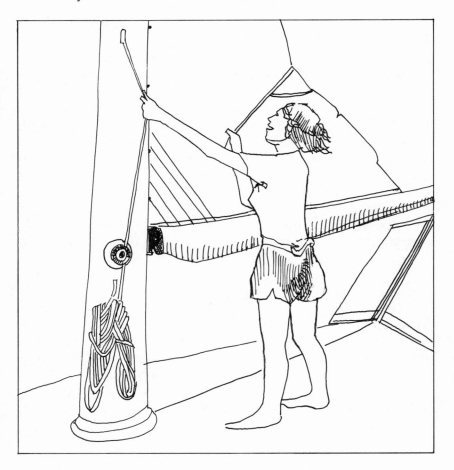

9
Rock-and-Roll, Boating Style

While wind is the most important ingredient to sailing, it can also be a nuisance. What you do, either the boat or the wind undoes—and fast!

If you launder your clothing and hang it carefully to dry on the lifelines, the wind will either steal it from you or blow it onto some filthy piece of equipment. So wipe down the lifelines and any rigging around where you plan to hang your clean clothing, and use lots of clothespins. And be prepared to wash it again if you are fortunate enough not to lose it overboard in a sudden strong gust of wind.

Belowdecks can be a bruising experience, especially in plunging seas. What you set down on any surface goes immediately to the floor. Stow all that you can into cupboards or deep holds, even if it looks securely tucked into a corner or outside shelf. In twelve-foot seas, nothing stays put. What is down jumps up. What is up falls down. What is on the port side smashes to starboard, and you can guess the rest.

Before you even set sail, perhaps while you are first motoring out and the seas are calm, check all of the cabinet and door latches belowdecks to make sure they lock securely. Tighten screws, bend out metal catches, and test all doors for safety before you find out that your soft drinks and beer are heavy enough to push out of their cabinets when you least want them to. Also, make sure that heavy cans or objects are not stacked up right behind the inside portion of the door clip. The clever devils learn quickly how to unlatch the door hooks from the inside.

You will notice right away that the sea consists of gallons and gallons of water. Some of that water prefers to ride inside your boat. Seawater is very creative and finds ways to come in you never dreamed it could. Test portholes and hatches before you sail. Take a hose and run pressurized water around the outside of your portholes (even if you must stand in a dinghy to do so). Be brutal! Try your best to get the water inside. Watch especially for dried out or broken rubber seals around the portholes and for cracks or missing bits of silicone caulking between the glass and metal.

While our boat was in the boatyard in Greece being fine-tuned for the Atlantic crossing, we were informed that all the caulking around the portholes was being replaced. When we hit our first big storm out in the Peloponnese, we discovered it had not been. We sponged, we wrung out, we bailed, we tried caulking; we sponged, wrung out and bailed some more. The crew grew so exhausted that the captain decided to find a quiet little anchorage at one of the islands we were passing and give us a rest. As there may not always be a handy bit of land where you can pull over and park, be sure you test for watertightness before you sail! You will find bailing most unpleasant when your vessel is plunging on its side through 30-knot winds and giant waves.

Find places away from the portholes to store anything you prefer to keep dry, like books, charts, papers, cassettes, etc. Articles stored in plastic or glass containers can withstand the sneaky seawater that would otherwise creep in no matter what else you have done to prevent it. Keep in mind that you probably cannot stop all the leaks, but slowing them down helps considerably.

Most boats are equipped with drawer stoppers to prevent the silverware and glasses from tumbling out when the boat is heeled over. If your boat has them, check each drawer carefully and be sure the stoppers are doing their job. If you don't have them, ask the captain if they can be installed. Flying knives and forks are not amusing.

Now, about your health and well-being. When on deck in rough seas, wear a harness attached to a through-bolted fitting or safety jacklines. If you're serious about sailing long passages, you may wish to invest in your own harness and life vest, especially if you'll be standing watch alone while others sleep. When you're on deck or belowdecks and the boat is underway, hang on with at least one hand as you move about.

As you work in the galley it's most important to become aware of the boat's movements and work with them. Stoves should be gimble-mounted, but nothing prevents boiling water from jumping out of the pots on occasion as the boat crashes and pounds over the waves (so don't fill pots to the top). Use pot-holders, aprons, and keep a cloth handy for constant wipe-ups.

Fruits and veggies purchased in bulk and stored for a long passage will roll around and rub against each other. Remember to turn your produce at least every two days and use immediately or throw out the badly bruised or slightly molded pieces. Potatoes, onions, and carrots will create their own condensation and the moisture will rot them fast. Pack newspapers around and between them and keep an eye on them.

Keep a frequent check on laundry hung on the lifelines in stiff winds. Bring it in as soon as it's dry to avoid sun bleaching.

If you know you'll be heading into rough seas, prepare sandwiches and thermos bottles of coffee, tea, and hot soup ahead of time. Stow the hot beverage containers in the deep galley sink and the sandwiches in the cold storage close to the top. Keep boxes of crackers or cookies and some chocolate bars handy as well. A favorite quick snack is cold baked potatoes! Life will be less frustrating and hazardous during rough weather if you do a bit of preparing ahead.

Be aware that you will be subjected to constant and often unpredictable motion. It's hard to detail all that you must do to protect yourself and your possessions from serious injury. A good idea is to sit down for a detailed discussion with the captain before you sail. Don't be afraid to ask questions or offer suggestions. Sometimes in the rush before sailing, the obvious can be overlooked. As soon as the boat starts moving, you'll discover what needs to be better secured. Think ahead and protect yourself and fellow crewmembers. Stow glassware, china, sharp objects, and anything breakable that's lying around after a prolonged stay in port.

You might think you're safe from harm while motoring along a quiet stretch of waterway. You might have a leisurely meal, wash the dishes, and leave them to dry on the counter top. But motoring down the Intracoastal Waterway in Florida, all it took was one discourteous powerboat operator to zoom past our boat and shatter our dishes and our afternoon in his violent wake. Assume that you will become the victim of someone's thoughtlessness, a sudden gust of wind, or a rogue wave—and put things away immediately after use.

The best rule of thumb while traveling on a constantly moving surface is to expect the unexpected. Keep a sharp eye out for potential hazards and act quickly to prevent damage or injury. A lot of jury-rigging is done during a passage; such temporary revisions can be undone quickly once you reach your cruising grounds. Use rags stuffed in drawers and doors. Use tape on surfaces that won't be damaged by adhesive. Rock-and-roll boating style is full of surprises!

10

Whither Thou Goest,
So Goest the Mail

When enjoying the sailing lifestyle you'll find that mail from family and friends is most welcome. Culture Shock can be quickly relieved by a warm, friendly letter. You'll be among crowds of people you don't know well, and sometimes surrounded by foreign languages you don't yet speak. And as you get deeper into your new lifestyle, you'll want news about your family, friends, and home country that can only come from mail while you're cruising.

All anchorages offer a mail station for visiting and cruising yachts. Once you arrive at a new destination where you plan to stay for two weeks or longer, you can ask any of the local yachties or someone at the marina office for information on where you can collect your mail.

If you know ahead of time where you're going, chances are the captain or some crewmember has been there before and can give you the mail-drop address. You can then send a note home from your current anchorage, or call to let your mail collector know where they can send your mail to greet you upon your arrival.

As mentioned earlier, American Express offices are rarely conveniently located for mail pick-up by yachties, except in certain areas of the Caribbean. Post offices, however, are often located right down at the water's edge, or not far therefrom. Having your mail sent to General Delivery, or Hold for Pick-up, with prior arrangements with the target post office, is a safe practice.

Yacht brokerages and charter agencies will most often cooperate and collect and hold your mail for your arrival. It's not a good practice to have your mail sent to an address without somehow informing someone there that it will be arriving.

Mentioned below are some locations and mail-drop addresses, but addresses do change. Double check the addresses and locations of each place before you arrive, or immediately upon arrival.

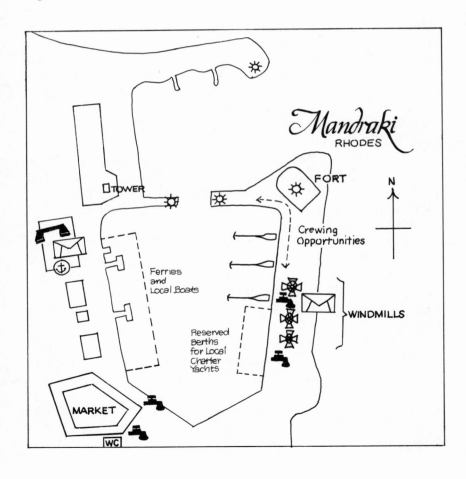

If you're cruising the Mediterranean, one place to go for mail is Mandraki Harbor, Rhodes. When I was there, windmill number three, right on the dock, was home for a charter agency that acted as a mail collection station for all visiting yachties. Upon your arrival, visit windmill number three (these are actual windmills on a rock shelf that divides the dock facilities from the ocean; you can't miss them) and let the agency know who you are and that you would like your mail sent to their address if they still perform that service. They will supply you with the proper address.

The primary location in Rhodes for mail pickup (a service performed for all visiting yachties) is:

Camper and Nicholson's Yacht Agency, Rhodes
26 Amerikis Street
P. O. Box 393
Rhodes, Greece

Be sure your mail is addressed to you in care of this address. C&N is up the hill past the marketplace, within easy walking distance from the harbor. Almost anyone asked can direct you.

In addition, should you crew for one or more of the various charter companies operating right out of Mandraki Harbor, you will most likely be able to pick up your mail at their office locations around town.

In Gibraltar, mail services are provided at Sheppard's Marina.

In the Caribbean there are quite a few places to collect your mail. In Grenada you will most likely pull into Prickly Bay to use their boatyard facilities, buy supplies, or just to visit a beautiful stopping point during your cruising. The Spice Island Marine Services boatyard office will act as a mail collection station for you. Let them know you would like to have your mail sent there, and then give out the following address to your mail forwarder:

Spice Island Marine Services
P. O. Box 449
Lance-aux-Epines
St. George's, Grenada, West Indies

If you are cruising farther up the chain of islands, you can also use The Boatyard Bar in Barbados (remember that all ARC racers and yachts crossing the Atlantic eventually stop here).

Another major mail collection station is English Harbour, Antigua. Have your mail sent in care of:

Nicholson's Yacht Charter
The Powder Magazine
English Harbour
Antigua, West Indies

Should you be cruising around the Virgin Islands, you might want to use the extensive facilities in the Ramada Inn Yacht Haven Marina in Charlotte Amalie harbor. The large, bright pink building complex is the gateway to the docking facilities. You can usually rent a mailbox at either the Charter Services or Flagship Services agency.

For yachts heading up to the United Kingdom from the Caribbean, mail can be picked up en route at Peter's Bar, Horta, the Azores.

Remember that names of organizations and their locations seem to change frequently, so it's advisable to check upon your arrival and be sure the service you choose plans to stay put long enough for you to receive your mail.

Wherever you travel, allow at least two weeks for mail delivery, and in remote areas like the South Pacific or the smaller islands in the Windward and Leeward chain of the Caribbean, up to a month.

Wherever you go, chat with seasoned yachties familiar with the area for the best and most convenient places to collect your mail. You should have no trouble in securing a convenient mail-collection location.

IN SUMMARY

Sailing is work. It can be, at times, frustrating and hair-raising, and serves up disappointments you never thought you would experience. But it also offers rewards beyond your wildest dreams. The lifestyle involves interesting people from all over the world sharing ideas and cultures. Sailing is teamwork. And education. And memories to last a lifetime.

To enter the sailing lifestyle you must plan carefully. Settle all personal business and outstanding bills. Organize your traveling paperwork. Protect your health. Save some money. Follow the procedures. Test your willingness to live on a boat offshore. Test your susceptibility to seasickness. Test your skills. Be prepared.

Pack only what you can carry—only what you need to survive. The luxuries and extras you'll find once you start crewing.

Be in the right place at the right time. Start with your local or nearest marinas. Talk to boat owners and other crewmembers. Follow the sailing seasons and remember where the boats float. Ask questions. Post notices. Mingle with the boating crowd.

Travel with a few solid skills like sewing, or mechanical repairs, or cooking, or just have some basic sailing knowledge. Keep yourself clean, trimmed and presentable. And smile—you're in for one exciting adventure after another.

Good sailing!

SAILING CHECKLIST

UNTANGLE YOUR TANGLE

—— Liquidate material possessions

—— Sell house or find responsible renter

—— Share rent with a roommate in less expensive accommodations

—— Give 30 days notice to landlord before moving out

—— Pay off all outstanding bills

—— Arrange with someone responsible to pay bills while traveling

—— Talk with tax accountant

—— Talk with investment counselor/Invest extra funds, if any

—— Apply for leave of absence at work or give notice

—— Arrange for someone responsible to collect mail

—— Store jewelry and other valuables

—— Stop shopping for anything but consumables

—— Change eating habits to simpler, healthier foods

—— Test yourself for seasickness and offshore living

REMEMBER: *If you cannot part with your material possessions and break your addictions, then the sailing life is not for you.*

GETTING YOUR DUCKS IN A ROW

—— Current passport

—— Visa information (read it, don't carry it)

—— International driver's license

—— Telephone company calling card (be sure to ask about calling restrictions from foreign countries)

—— Start inoculations two months before departure date

—— Photocopy passport, driver's license, health record, and leave copies with someone responsible

———— Arrange with family or friends to use their mailing address

———— Leave small sum of money on account with credit card company to charge against

———— Set up joint or individual personal checking account with minimum of $1,000

———— Set up personal passbook savings account with minimum of $5,000

———— Purchase $2,000 in traveler's checks

———— Get prescription for seasickness prevention patches (if necessary)

———— Pack passport

———— Pack inoculation record

———— Pack checkbook and traveler's checks

———— Pack one major credit card

———— Pack telephone company calling card (optional)

———— Read basic sailing instruction book

REMEMBER: *Leave copies of important documents behind. Be prepared to act as unofficial ambassador for "home country." Make a good impression.*

LUGGAGE BEARERS WON'T BE NEEDED

———— Gather items on basic clothing list (lightweight, fast-drying)

———— Gather items on personal products list (non-greasy creams, plastic bottles)

———— Gather items on first-aid kit list

———— Gather items on miscellaneous items list

———— Measure items to be packed for correct seabag size

———— Purchase sturdy foldable seabag

———— Purchase small padlock and key for seabag

———— Purchase small canvas carry-on bag (lock optional)

REMEMBER: *Do not overpack! Do not pack or carry more than you can comfortably handle by yourself.*

YOU'LL NEED A LITTLE MONEY

——— Purchase round-trip, open-return airline ticket

——— Reserve a room in city where search is to begin

——— Use charge card for hotels, meals (where possible), rental cars

——— Use traveler's checks, local currency for buses, taxis, postage, telephone calls, medical/dental, miscellaneous purchases

——— Exchange currency in small amounts

——— Exchange currency only in banks unless in emergency

——— Spend local currency earned in same country as earned

——— Leave all loose change in country of origin

——— Apply for additional traveler's checks in major bank one week before needed

——— Record all earnings and keep for tax reporting

REMEMBER: *Do not enter this lifestyle unless you can afford to pay your own way on land in between crewing assignments.*

WHERE THE BOATS FLOAT

The West Coast of the United States

——— Pacific Northwest

——— San Francisco

——— San Diego

The East Coast of the United States

——— Florida

The Caribbean

——— Barbados

——— Bequia—Elizabeth Harbour and Lower Bay

——— St. Thomas—Charlotte Amalie Harbor

The Mediterranean

——— Rhodes, Greece—Mandraki Harbor

------ Turkey—Marmaris and Fethye

Gibraltar

------ Sheppard's Marina, Marina Bay, The Anchorage

FIND CREWING POSITIONS BY

------ Walking the docks at pleasure marinas

------ Asking "do you need crew?"

------ Asking for referrals

------ Posting "crew available" notices

------ Registering with crewfinding agencies

------ Frequenting yachtie hangouts

REMEMBER: *If you don't ask, you won't get!*

WHO SAYS YOU CAN'T COOK?

------ Learn to boil water

------ Tell the truth about your level of cooking skills

------ Buy a good sailing cookbook and take it with you

------ Practice some recipes

------ Keep meals simple

REMEMBER: *You can always sign on as deckhand.*

YO HO HO, A PIRATE'S LIFE

------ Learn marine toilet operation on each boat

------ Conserve water on board

------ Separate biodegradable from non-biodegradable garbage

------ Keep the boat shipshape, clean up clutter

------ Be a sensitive, caring host/hostess

------ Learn to be a smart shopper when provisioning

———— Learn how to operate boat's electrical systems

———— Learn how to operate the boat's engine

———— Learn basic sailing terminology

REMEMBER: *A little knowledge and experience can go a long way.*

ROCK-AND-ROLL, BOATING STYLE

———— Be alert for wind nuisance

———— Take care when working belowdecks

———— Hang on when on deck or wear a safety harness

———— Expect the unexpected

REMEMBER: *Working on a boat means constant, unpredictable motion.*

WHITHER THOU GOEST, SO GOEST THE MAIL

———— Ask about mail collection stations upon arrival if you plan a long stay

———— Verify with mail station that you can receive mail there

———— Call or write your mail collector with your address

———— Stay put long enough for mail to reach you (minimum 2 weeks)

REMEMBER: *Have a good time! Sailing is fun.*